HERMES BOOKS

John Herington, General Editor

Also available in this series:

Homer, by Paolo Vivante (1985)
Pindar, by D. S. Carne-Ross (1985)
Aeschylus, by John Herington (1986)

HESIOD

ROBERT LAMBERTON

YALE UNIVERSITY PRESS
NEW HAVEN AND LONDON

Designed by Sally Harris
and set in Palatino type by
Brevis Press, Bethany, Connecticut.
Printed in the United States of America by
Vail-Ballou Press, Binghamton, New York.

Library of Congress Cataloging-in-Publication Data

Lamberton, Robert
  Hesiod.

  (Hermes books)
  Bibliography: p.
  Includes index.
    I. Hesiod—Criticism and interpretation.
2. Mythology, Greek, in literature.   3. Greece
in literature.   I. Title.
PA4011.L36   1988   881′.01   87–10595
ISBN 0–300–04068–7 (alk. paper)
ISBN 0–300–04069–5 (pbk.)

The paper in this book meets the guidelines for
permanence and durability of the Committee on
Production Guidelines for Book Longevity
of the Council on Library Resources.

10   9   8   7   6   5   4   3   2   1

FOR SUSAN

CONTENTS

FOREWORD

"It would be a pity," said Nietzsche, "if the classics should speak to us less clearly because a million words stood in the way." His forebodings seem now to have been realized. A glance at the increasing girth of successive volumes of the standard journal of classical bibliography, *L'Année Philologique*, since World War II is enough to demonstrate the proliferation of writing on the subject in our time. Unfortunately, the vast majority of the studies listed will prove on inspection to be largely concerned with points of detail and composed by and for academic specialists in the field. Few are addressed to the literate but nonspecialist adult or to that equally important person, the intelligent but uninstructed beginning student; and of those few, very few indeed are the work of scholars of the first rank, equipped for their task not merely with raw classical erudition but also with style, taste, and literary judgment.

It is a strange situation. On one side stand the classical masters of Greece and Rome, those models of concision, elegance, and understanding of the human condition, who composed least of all for narrow technologists, most of all for the Common Reader (and, indeed, the Common Hearer). On the other side stands a sort of industrial complex, processing those masters into an annually growing output of technical articles and monographs. What is lacking, it seems, in our society as well as in our scholarship, is the kind of book that

was supplied for earlier generations by such men as Richard
Jebb and Gilbert Murray in the intervals of their more technical researches—the kind of book that directed the general
reader not to the pyramid of secondary literature piled over
the burial places of the classical writers but to the living faces
of the writers themselves, as perceived by a scholar-humanist
with a deep knowledge of, and love for, his subject. Not only
for the sake of the potential student of classics, but also for
the sake of the humanities as a whole, within and outside
academe, it seems that this gap in classical studies ought to
be filled. The Hermes series is a modest attempt to fill it.

We have sought men and women possessed of a rather
rare combination of qualities: a love for literature in other
languages, extending into modern times; a vision that extends
beyond academe to contemporary life itself; and above all an
ability to express themselves in clear, lively, and graceful English, without polysyllabic language or parochial jargon. For
the aim of the series requires that they should communicate
to nonspecialist readers, authoritatively and vividly, their personal sense of why a given classical author's writings have
excited people for centuries and why they can continue to do
so. Some are classical scholars by profession, some are not;
each has lived long with the classics, and especially with the
author about whom he or she writes in this series.

The first, middle, and last goal of the Hermes series is to
guide the general reader to a dialogue with the classical masters rather than to acquaint him or her with the present state
of scholarly research. Thus our volumes contain few or no
footnotes; even within the texts, references to secondary literature are kept to a minimum. At the end of each volume,
however, is a short bibliography that includes recommended
English translations, and selected literary criticism, as well
as historical and (when appropriate) biographical studies.

Throughout, all quotations from the Greek or Latin texts are given in English translation.

In these ways we hope to let the classics speak again, with a minimum of modern verbiage (as Nietzsche wished), to the widest possible audience of interested people.

John Herington

WHAT HESIOD MIGHT HAVE SAID AS HE RECEIVED
INSPIRATION FROM THE MUSES ON HELIKON

What goddess has shaken me, what divine inspiration leads me
to leave the shadowy mountains and the flocks?
What goddess in a single night taught me to cut
thick boughs of the rich laurel of Helikon?
Tell me now of the families of gods and the wars of giants,
the genealogies of all the heroes and the race of women.
Tell me a world never seen by my eyes.
Too bad for my poor sheepfold and my pens of goats.
I go forth to the cities, the marketplaces and the contests.
The sacred ivy and the flock no longer satisfy me.
The whole of Askra with its wretched huts stifles me.
Not even Kyme itself would interest me. Farewell,
all you shepherds! The Muses have taught me the holy song
and I have drawn a great flood from the spring of Aganippe.
Now Dios, dearest father, now Pykimede,
proud mother, and Perses, you big fool,
you will set up . . .   . . . for I shall not
set out to sing a paltry shepherd's song, or what
sunburned peasants sing. . . .
The goatherd's flute is not for me.
I despise the wild sound and the reed pipes.
From Zeus, from the Muses . . .   . . . the gates of the heavens
appear before me—I see into the divine mansions.
And now I will sing. . . .

[A reconstruction (true to the spirit, if not, perhaps, to the letter) of a
poem preserved in fragmentary form on a damaged papyrus (Pap. Oxy.
3537r). The Greek original is said to date from the third or fourth century
of our era.]

PREFACE

HESIOD, FROM OUR PERSPECTIVE, MAY BE THE MOST IMPORTANT of ancient authors. This in itself is a paradox. Hesiod has been considered a poet of the first rank only during a few brief periods in the history of European literature. But he is our principal source for the earliest recorded phase of Greek ideas about the gods and the relations of gods and men. If this were not enough, he also gives us what appears to be the first picture of the society and economy of rural Greece as it emerged from the dark age that separates European prehistory from European history. (If I seem to neglect Homer, it is because he pretends to represent a much earlier age, and even to the extent that he may be seen to portray contemporary reality he has no precedence over Hesiod.)

The reading of Hesiod offered here does not stress his value as a historical, mythological, or theological source, although these issues are fraught with difficulties that require at least a provisional resolution in order for the poems to be read. What I have attempted is to set various elements in perspective by a reading of the poems themselves. As will rapidly become clear, we are lacking certain information that we would dearly love to have at hand to serve as background for such a reading. There has been doubt since antiquity regarding the authenticity of various parts of the Hesiodic corpus—doubt not simply about which poems were Hesiod's but about which lines even of the *Theogony* and the *Works and Days* were authentic. The contributions of our own century have placed the very existence of the poet Hesiod in doubt, emphasizing both the credulity of those who have taken the autobiographical material in the poems at face value and the traditional and conventional nature of archaic Greek poetry. Accepting the impossibility of demonstrating conclusively the historicity or nonhistoricity of Hesiod, I have attempted to take what we know about the Hesiodic corpus, tempered by what we do not know, and to arrive at a way of making sense of what we have.

To acknowledge the debts of this little book would require a long list, especially in view of the limits on bibliography imposed by the format of the series. Nevertheless, a few names should stand here simply because these people's contributions to its genesis have been so great. Among recent writers on Hesiod and on archaic Greek poetry in general, I am everywhere indebted to M. L. West and Gregory Nagy. The bibliographical note suggests the significance of their contributions and points to other important recent work. The translation of the third- or fourth-century poem on the page facing this preface incorporates supplements proposed by P. J. Parsons and M. L. West as well as one of my own. Ellen Graham saw the book through the Press, and her helpful suggestions along with Laura Jones Dooley's skillful editorial work have contributed substantially to its final form. A. M. Snodgrass received me warmly at Mavromati in Boeotia and shared the results of his survey work in the Valley of the Muses. Other debts are of a personal nature, to friends, colleagues, and scholars who have aided me in my work on Hesiod in various ways too complex to spell out here. To list only those to whom I am most indebted, sincere thanks to Alan Cameron, Steve Diamant, Richard Janko, David Jordan, John Herington, Piero Pucci, and, as always, Susan Rotroff.

HESIOD

I HESIOD AND THE HESIODIC TRADITION

The Hesiodic Persona: Confession, Convention, and Myth

And as for the tripod Hesiod consecrated to Apollo on
Helikon . . . that should be preserved in the museum
of imposture [*nel museo dell'impostura*].
—Giambattista Vico, *La scienza nuova* (1744), 97

I have looked very carefully into the question of the
dates of Homer and Hesiod, but I would rather not
write on this matter, since I know how quarrelsome
those who study epic poetry are, especially of late.
—Pausanius (9.30.3)

FROM BEFORE THE TIME OF PERIKLES UNTIL OUR OWN CEN-
tury, it was largely accepted by those who looked to archaic
Greece for the precedents and sources of the European tradition in literature that at some remote time a Boetian shepherd named Hesiod met the nine daughters of Memory, the
Muses, on Mount Helikon and, thanks to their tutelage, was
able to compose two poems. In one, the *Theogony,* he provided
an account of the gods of the Greeks, their origins, relationships, and powers, which was as nearly definitive and canonical as a theological tradition that was notoriously the
property of poets and liars could permit. In the other, the
Works and Days, he laid out instructions for the small land-
holder to guide him through the agricultural year. This figure

1

of Hesiod the rustic bard was modified, of course, from generation to generation. The Muses might be taken as poetic personifications of the qualities of the poet's art, goddesses only as a function of his self-gratulatory hyperbole—indeed, Hesiod's own language encourages us to understand them in this way. The pastoral landscape that served as his backdrop might be variously conceived, though here in fact there is remarkable continuity from the Hellenistic period to the eighteenth century, when pastoral as a genre was swallowed up in irony and in the smoke and soot of the industrial revolution. The figure of the poet remained, however, largely intact, and even when pastoral poetry as such was no longer thinkable the shepherd Hesiod survived, a historical entity whose place in the history books was as secure as that of any other personage of the archaic period.

In the past generation or two, however, research on the nature of oral tradition has severely reduced our ability to regard that figure as historical, and much that could have been said with confidence about Hesiod fifty years ago has now only the status of lost certainties. Lost certainties are dangerous. Men and women of science are very sensitive to those dangers, and they immediately banish fallen truths— now falsehoods—to the realm of the irrelevant and uninteresting. But those who are concerned with cultural traditions cannot be so rash. Hesiod as conceived by the Romans, by the Elizabethans, by the eighteenth century, has from our perspective nearly the importance of the elusive entity we can provisionally call our own Hesiod. If recent research has undermined a coherent picture developed and refined by more than eighty generations of tradition, we cannot begin to come to terms with Hesiod for ourselves without first fully appreciating that picture and the power it has had over the imagination.

Let us, then, before saying what little we can about the author or authors of the *Theogony* and the *Works and Days*, pause to look at the history of what we may call the Hesiodic persona, the "mask," or vehicle, of the poetry. Our reasons for distinguishing between this mask and the poet himself will become clearer as we proceed. In the most general terms, we may describe the contents of the *Theogony* and the *Works and Days* as myths, traditional tales available for elaboration and use by poets and artists. What we are about to look at— the events of Hesiod's life, his contest with Homer, and so forth—are Hesiodic myths of another sort, myths that provide a vehicle for the Hesiodic tales of gods and heroes (cf. Nagy 1982).

The figure of Hesiod the rustic bard is based, ultimately, on a few bits of sketchy but emphatic and unambiguous information supplied by the poems themselves. These primary data were elaborated at an early date into short biographies, fleshed out either by more-or-less authentic traditions or, just as likely, by the creative imaginations of the biographers. The information poems provide about their creators is notoriously unreliable, and literary biography in antiquity was largely an exercise in the reworking of such information into explanatory tales, ancillary to the poems themselves. These biographical sketches complemented the poems by providing ready answers to a complex of questions that were themselves traditional expressions of the relationship—and the distance— between the audience of the poem and its creator. The emperor Hadrian asked the Oracle at Delphi, "Where was Homer born? Who was his father?" Others added such questions as "What sort of man was he? Where did he die?" These questions should be understood as interrogations intimately bound up with the mysterious power of poetry (and especially traditional poetry), as attempts to reduce something of superhuman scale (and as such conventionally called "divine") to the format of a finite life, a curriculum vitae, a list of vital statistics.

Even in antiquity, some of the mythic elements in the lives of the poets were recognized for what they are, at least by literary scholars of the sophistication and the predilection for allegory of the Neoplatonist Proklos (who died about A.D. 485). Here is the beginning of his account of Hesiod:

> Hesiod and his brother Perses were the children of Dios and Pykimede, themselves poor people from Aeolian Kyme [on the Aegean coast of Asia Minor].
>
> Out of poverty and need they left their home in Kyme and moved to Askra, a Boeotian village lying at the foot of Mt. Helikon, with a bad climate both winter and summer, and settled there. These people were so poor that Hesiod tended sheep on Mt. Helikon. They say that nine women came and cut Helikonian laurel branches and gave them to him to eat, and thus he was filled with wisdom and poetry.
>
> This much is sound and perfectly true, that Hesiod was the son of Dios and Pykimede and he tended sheep on Helikon. The rest is mythic and meant allegorically.

Proklos goes on to explain the allegory, emphasizing the idea that Hesiod's promotion from shepherd to poet is first of all a variant of the rags-to-riches (or at least rags-to-fame) story and that the nine ladies' gift of bitter laurel represents the bitter toil of education that permitted his rise. In more concrete terms, the "speaking laurel of Helikon" represents the books over which he toiled. Proklos's interpretation is a bit stilted, oversimplified, and lacking in persuasive force. It is nevertheless very modern in its perception that poets' biographies like this one have a special structure of meaning.

They are secondary myths generated by the tradition of the poems themselves.

The biographies of Hesiod may be reduced to four central episodes: his genealogy, his vision on Mount Helikon, his competition with Homer, and the circumstances of his death. With genealogy is bound up the question of date, and the lack of agreement within the tradition on this point (a problem noted repeatedly from Herodotos to Proklos and the Byzantine writers) is perhaps the strongest indication we have that the Hesiod of the biographies is largely a figure of convention. The early Pythagoreans, who believed in metempsychosis, established the technique of explaining the poetic tradition in terms of the repeated incarnations of certain privileged souls. Thus Stesikhoros could be said to be a reincarnation of Homer, both of them expressions in the flesh of the same transcendent vision. The genealogies evoked in the poetic biographies often serve the same function, drawing the poet into definable relationships with gods and other poets and replacing reincarnation with heredity.

While Proklos accepts without comment the traditional names given to Hesiod's parents, he rejects the rest, passing over in silence the genealogies that trace the ancestry of Homer and Hesiod to Apollo and Poseidon by way of Orpheus. One goal of these fantastic genealogies was to make of Homer and Hesiod both relatives and contemporaries, in order to accommodate the legend of their competition—a legend which, though rejected as an anachronistic fabrication by some ancient literary historians, was both widespread and popular.

The tale of the competition between the two poets who stood at the source of the Greek tradition is preserved primarily through a text known as the *Certamen*, or *Contest of Homer and Hesiod*, itself no earlier than the time of the Emperor

Hadrian, who died in A.D. 138. The story, however, is much older, attested four centuries earlier in a fragmentary Ptolemaic papyrus and doubtless to be traced right back to the archaic period. The surviving version incorporates a variety of themes borrowed from early epic itself. The funeral games of a Euboean king form the appropriately heroic context for the competition (usually referred to as an *eris*, "strife" or "conflict," a word with strong Homeric and Hesiodic associations). Like most of the biographical elaborations, this one starts from the text. In general terms, the idea might well have arisen from the list of examples Hesiod chooses to illustrate the action of the good eris, or competition, in the *Works and Days* (25–26):

> Potter fights with potter, carpenter with carpenter,
> beggar is jealous of beggar, bard of bard.

But more specifically the contest takes its clue from Hesiod's description of his own single sea-voyage, from Aulis (*W&D* 654–57):

> Thence I set forth for the funeral games of brilliant
>   Amphidamus
> in Khalkis. Vast prizes were announced,
> offered by his greathearted sons. It is my boast
> that there I was victorious in song and carried off the
>   eared tripod.

Pausanias, the second-century A.D. traveler, certainly knew this version of *Works and Days* 657 and says that he saw the tripod in question when he visited the slopes of Mount Helikon. But another version, preserved in an ancient marginal note to the poem, made this Hesiod's boast:

> that there, in Khalkis, I defeated divine Homer in song.

As we shall see, it is one of the paradoxes in the study of archaic Greek poetic tradition that we are ill equipped to choose between alternate versions of this sort. We may say here that the variant represents a corruption of the "original" text of the *Works and Days* by a "later" poet in the tradition, one who seeks to establish explicitly in the text the justification for a subsequent elaboration (the competition of Homer and Hesiod) previously fabricated on the basis of this same passage in its original form. But as we say this, we should be aware that other formulations are possible and that cause and effect are difficult to separate here. The secondary mythical-biographical tradition has very much the same relationship to the text of Hesiod that invertebrate parasites have to higher organisms: every evolutionary change in the latter opens up new ecological niches, new opportunities, for the former to exploit. We have good reason to believe that the evolution of the text of Hesiod was a long and complex process, repeatedly interacting with the biographical tradition in ways we are no longer able to reconstruct with confidence.

In the *Contest* as we have it, Hesiod and Homer first perform a duet consisting of improvised questions posed by Hesiod and answered by Homer, who sometimes quotes himself and sometimes improvises. Frustrated by Homer's skill and wit, Hesiod proceeds to a type of contest known to have been popular in the classical period at symposia, or drinking parties. In response to a line posed by the questioner, the answerer must produce a line that matches it metrically and syntactically and extends or completes the sense. Again Homer cannot be intimidated and ingeniously counters everything Hesiod can propose, and then with equal wit answers another series of questions, at the end of which the audience calls for Homer to receive the prize. The judge overrules them, however, and calls for the contest to continue with each bard performing what he himself considers best from his own work. Hesiod opens with his description of the May harvest (*W&D* 383ff.) and Homer counters with a rousing battle prelude (*Il.* 13.126ff.), and again the audience cheers for Homer. (Proklos's account adds at this point that it was the "nobles and soldiers" who applauded.) The king nevertheless overturns the audience's decision and awards the prize to Hesiod, "claiming that it was right for the poet who encouraged his audience toward farming and peace to win, and not the one who described war and slaughter" (*Contest* 322). The important thing is not, of course, the pseudo-historical context but rather the very real contrast between Homeric and Hesiodic poetry developed here, and the king's dilemma is a genuine and enduring one. He must choose between Homer's more attractive, rousing poetry—the clear winner if only aesthetic considerations are admitted—and Hesiod's poetry with its greater social utility. The author of the *Contest* is telling us that Homer brings greater immediate pleasure, perhaps even that war is simply more interesting than farming (at least as subject matter for art), but that Hesiod is better for society and that a good administrator would have to crown the latter. It is precisely the traditional judgment expressed in this little fable that informs Sokrates' systematic critique of Homer in Plato's *Republic*. For purposes of the fable, Homer and Hesiod become symbolic of two genres, two modes of early hexameter poetry: heroic military epic on the one hand, and wisdom poetry with its rural setting on the other. As we shall see, this reductionist schematization may well be simply the mythic expression of the actual historical process that produced the Homeric corpus and the Hesiodic corpus.

The *Contest* tells us that Hesiod was the victor over Homer, but his victory is posed as a paradox, a victory that is deserved only if viewed from a certain perspective, which is not that of most audiences of poetry. It is balanced by the final episode in this exercise in imaginative biography, the story of Hesiod's death. After the undeserved triumph in the contest comes an undeserved death sentence at the hands of well-meaning but deluded hosts who believe Hesiod to have seduced their sister. The episode is introduced through the familiar device of the misleading oracle. The Pythia in Delphi promises Hesiod eternal fame and advises him to avoid "the beautiful grove of Nemean Zeus." Following her instructions, he avoids the place obviously designated, the site of the Nemean games in the Peloponnisos, and travels from Delphi in the opposite direction, to a place in Lokris called Oinoe. But like the well-meaning Oedipus, Hesiod only compounds his troubles. Oinoe turns out to be a little-known shrine of Nemean Zeus, and the poet's hosts there murder him and throw his body into the sea, from which it is returned three days later by dolphins. This dolphin motif echoes a story that was told to explain the hero shrine of Palaimon at the site of the Isthmian games. The association of Hesiod with hero shrines is reinforced by the further story of the removal of the poet's bones to Minyan Orkhomenos (in Boetia, not far from Mount Helikon) in obedience to an oracle. Corresponding stories are told of Homer's death, including the motif of the anticipatory oracle, though in Hesiod's case the biographer's debt to the Oedipus story is more conspicuous. All of this body of material has the look of local history of the sort Pausanias has collected—stories told in Lokris or at Orkhomenos (or in Homer's case, on Ios) to explain an ancient and revered monument or cult. We have no real reason to believe that Hesiod's bones were ever deposited in a hero shrine, and indeed the evidence for a cult of Homer has been greatly exaggerated as well. The *Contest* makes it crystal clear, though, that the biographical tradition *wanted* us to believe that these poets were the objects of cults, and, given the fact that these secondary myths had the function of enhancing the prestige of the body of poetry which generated them (a process clearly visible within the poems as well, in the poets' self-advertisements), we need not assume the existence of actual cults.

This brief survey has covered most of the givens on the life and cultural context of Hesiod. All seem ultimately to be derived from hints or claims made in the poems themselves (though local traditions in Boeotia and elsewhere may have been the sources of some motifs) and to have been elaborated by the biographers to the greater glory of the poet. Hesiod's autobiographical bent is often contrasted with the carefully preserved anonymity of the Homeric narrative voice. Nowhere in the Homeric corpus except in an aside in the *Hymn to Delian Apollo* does the narrative voice reveal anything of its source, and the single reference there to "the blind man from rocky Khios, whose songs are forever the finest" (172–73) constitutes the lone point of contact between the Homeric corpus and the parallel biographical tradition. This difference between Hesiod and Homer is a real one, but its significance is easily exaggerated. The name Hesiod in fact occurs in the corpus only once (*Theog.* 22), and even there it is possible to doubt whether it designates the speaker. The brother, Perses, with whom the speaker of the *Works and Days* is in dispute over inherited land, is mentioned ten times (always in formulas of address), and their father once (*W&D* 633). To conclude that we have in Hesiod a poet who, in contrast to the anonymous Homeric narrator, incorporates his identity fully into his work and gives us the specificity of an individual personality and biography would be mistaken. What we do have here (and this will become clearer later) is a poetic tradition parallel to the Homeric one—a parallelism that the secondary myths express as competition—in which a greater variety of traditional material draws along with it a greater variety of traditional modes of diction and convention for dealing with that material.

The Hesiodic Corpus and Oral Composition

These are his works: Theogony, Shield [of Herakles], Catalogue of the Women of the Heroic Period (in 5 books), a dirge (for someone named Batrakhos, with whom he was in love), On the Idaean Dactyls, and many others.

—*The Suda*

The ancients seem not to agree with one another regarding the number of the children of Niobe. . . . Hesiod says there were 19, unless the verses are not Hesiod's at all, but like many others have been mistakenly attributed to him.

—Aelian, *Varia Historia*, 12.36

Hesiod is a name that from the sixth century before Christ (and perhaps earlier) has been attached to a substantial body of archaic and archaizing Greek poetry. If anything in the Greek tradition was to be considered as old (and therefore as worthy of respect) as the poems of Homer, it was the body of poetry traditionally attributed to Hesiod. Orpheus and Mousaios lived somewhat earlier, according to some, but Homer and Hesiod were canonical. At the same time, as Aelian (writing about A.D. 200) indicates, it has been clear to sensitive readers since antiquity that much of that disparate material could not be realistically attributed to a single poet.

Tremendous advances within the field of the study of archaic Greek poetry have, within the past half-century, radically altered our view of this question and our expectations regarding the possibility of a solution. Both the Hesiodic Question and its better known cousin, the Homeric Question, could be conceived two generations ago as soluble, though difficult, problems, analogous to similar ones in more recent literary history. We can say with some certainty what are and are not the poems of, say, Wordsworth. As we push farther back, to Shakespeare, for example, the problems become greater but not insoluble. Areas within the Shakespearean corpus are open to dispute, and the collaborations pose special problems, yet we are confident that the truth lies there somewhere. A given verse either *is* or *is not* Shakespeare's, and our experts in the field are capable of a reasonable approximation of the truth.

Until this century it was possible to approach the definition of the oeuvres of the earliest Greek poets in the same way. Of course, the literature of Greece and Rome is riddled with pseudepigrapha created for a variety of motives. Perhaps the most striking example is the body of poetry called the *Anakreontea*, the bulk of it claiming, with whatever seriousness, to be the work of the sixth-century B.C. lyric poet Anakreon, a contemporary of Polykrates of Samos and the Peisistratids of Athens, of whom we know (or are given by tradition) a number of biographical details. When a substantial body of Anakreontic poetry was discovered in a Byzantine anthology and published in the West in 1554, it rapidly gained tremendous popularity, especially among the group of French poets known as the Pléiade, and was treated as a major recovery of archaic poetry. It gradually became clear to philologists, however, that the bulk of this elegant erotic poetry was not archaic at all but Hellenistic and even Byzantine. Anakreon, it seemed, had plied his trade for over a millennium, or, rather, he had created a tradition, an enduring persona or poetic identity, that was adopted again and again by later poets. Here is the perfect example of the author as trope of the poem. These poets were not counterfeiters, if the definition of that crime involves intent to deceive. Rather, they resembled those nineteenth- and twentieth-century violin makers who used the patterns and templates of Guarneri and Stradivari and even inserted labels bearing the great makers' names—*not* in order to deceive their customers (though many have since been deceived in ignorance of the convention) but simply to identify the model, the archetype that was followed, recreated, and realized in their own creation. The followers of Anakreon did the same; they sang *as* Anakreon. The identification of the speaking voice of the poem with that of the archaic poet was a convention and so a condition of their genre. The creator of the poem that serves as epigraph to this volume was similarly engaged in speaking through the mask of Hesiod, the shepherd of Mount Helikon, roughly a millennium after the time tradition tells us the "real" Hesiod tended his flock.

In speaking of Anakreon, we are concerned with a body of poetry which, though certainly conceived for performance rather than private reading, belongs to a fully literate context. We have to push back still further to reach Hesiod, and in so doing we find ourselves approaching the limits of literacy in the Greek world, and with those limits a radically different conception of poetic tradition and its relationship to its social context. It is generally (though by no means universally) accepted that the adaptation of the Phoenician alphabet to Greek, and consequently the beginning of Greek alphabetic literacy, falls within the eighth century B.C. The earliest surviving alphabetically written Greek is a graffito on a pot manufactured about 740 B.C. (though perhaps inscribed later), and it has been argued on the basis of what can be reconstructed of the evolution of the phonetic values and shapes of the Phoenician letters that the adaptation is unlikely to go back earlier than approximately 825 (though here again much earlier dates have been plausibly brought forward).

What can we say about the date of Hesiod? As we have seen, the biographical tradition is more concerned with his relative than his absolute date and dissolves into contradictions in its attempts to make him prior to, contemporary with, or later than Homer. A similar disagreement prevailed in ancient discussion of the date of Homer relative to the Trojan War, which we conventionally place in the thirteenth or twelfth century and to which some insisted Homer was an eyewitness. There was, however, a tradition regarding the absolute date of the two poets that went back to Herodotos, writing about 450, who estimated that Homer and Hesiod lived "not more than four hundred years" before his own time and who went on to claim that such poets as Orpheus whom tradition placed still earlier were in fact later (*Hist.* 2.53). For Herodotos, then, Homer and Hesiod marked the beginning of Greek poetry (and hence of Greek theology), and though he was surely ignorant of the chronology of the coming of literacy to Greece, Herodotos placed these two poets at a time immediately preceding what is today generally viewed as the dawn of Greek literacy. Herodotos's date is too early by modern standards, and we cannot claim that it was ever generally accepted. The life of Hesiod in the Byzantine lexicon called *The Suda* summed up the opinions of the ancients as follows: "According to some, he was older than Homer, and according to others, his contemporary. Porphyry and most of the others make him younger by a hundred years, so as to place him only 32 years before the first Olympiad [= 776 B.C.]."

This would give us Homer active about 900 (too early again) and Hesiod reaching his peak just before 800, still too early, but not by so much. The most respectable modern opinions on the date of the *Theogony* range from the last quarter of the eighth century (M. L. West) to the second quarter of the seventh (G. S. Kirk), that is, within the century or so just *after* the apparent introduction of alphabetic literacy in Greece.

The ancient scholars, then, in their ignorance both of the relationship of early poetry to oral tradition and of the date of the introduction of writing in Greece, conceived both Homer and Hesiod as individual creative personalities and gave them various dates all of which fall before the time when we can realistically imagine there to have been Greek poets who composed their poems in writing. Recent scholars, on the other hand, with considerably more understanding of the chronology of ancient Greece, tend to place both poets in the first century and a half of Greek alphabetic literacy. Certainty is not to be hoped for, though methodological innovations are constantly increasing our ability to make fine distinctions within the field of archaic hexameter poetry. What we can say with some certainty is that the *Iliad*, the *Odyssey*, the *Theogony*, and the *Works and Days* were written down sometime between the beginning of alphabetic literacy in Greece and the latter part of the sixth century. Paradoxically, though, we are not in a position to explain clearly the relationship between the composition of these poems and their recording in writing, nor do we know how closely the poems we have resemble the ones recorded in the early centuries of Greek literacy. Our uncertainties on this score result from the demonstration, some fifty years ago, that archaic Greek hexameter poetry was born in an oral rather than a literate context.

The story of Milman Parry's work on Serbo-Croatian oral epic and his demonstration of the oral nature of Homeric verse has often been told (see Kirk 1962a; Lord 1960). Still, since that work constitutes the watershed separating the traditional Hesiod—Hesiod the shepherd of Helikon—from any account of the origin of Hesiodic poetry viable for our own time, the essentials of Parry's contribution must be recalled here. Parry showed that Homer's poetic vocabulary of formulas, or fixed phrases, as well as his narrative procedures, were diagnostic signs of oral composition. Of particular importance are the relationships of the formulaic phrases among themselves; groups of similar formulas develop by extension to occupy various parts of the line and observe a principle of economy—that is, interchangeable formulas (metrically identical formulas of roughly the same meaning) generally do not exist for the same position in the line. By studying a living tradition of oral epic song in Yugoslavia, Parry concluded that the poetic language of Homer could not possibly be considered the creation of a single man but rather must have evolved through the tiny, immeasurable contributions of many bards over a number of generations. He further concluded that a vital, creative tradition of oral epic was not compatible with literacy on the part of the singers.

The Homeric Question seemed to dissolve in a flash. To determine whether the *Iliad* and *Odyssey* had the same author was no longer a serious goal. Both had many authors—or rather the conditions of their telling, of their composition, presupposed the labors of generations of bards, building a vast vocabulary of stock expressions and narrative motifs that found fullest realization in these great epics.

Much subsequent discussion of "Parryism"—predictably, the problems raised by Parry's discoveries have generated heated controversy—have been ideologically determined, though the preconceptions of the two camps have never been made explicit. What Parry had done was to demonstrate the oral and traditional *background* of Homeric poetry. He had not shown how the poems as we have them came first to exist, and then to be committed to writing. There was resistance to the idea that poems of the scale and complexity of the *Iliad* and *Odyssey* could possibly have been realized within such an oral tradition. Surely a master poet must be postulated at the end of the oral line, one who either learned to write or dictated his supreme achievement(s). The poetic language as well as the content might be traditional—this seems to be accepted on all sides—but the final organization, the manipulation of that traditional language in *these* poems, with their exquisite detail and rich thematic texture on a scale extending far beyond the possibilities of any single bardic performance, all of this, the "anti-Parry" camp has claimed, must be traced to a single personality, a single genius. In its belated, far more sophisticated way, the "anti-Parry" camp has gone back to the questions about Homer that Hadrian addressed to the Pythia.

The final implications of "Parryism" leave us with a poem without a poet, a group of masterpieces lying at the very sources of the European tradition of literature that are in fact something fundamentally different from anything else in that tradition (if we ignore for the moment the later contributions of vernacular oral poetry in the Middle Ages). These poems, which from antiquity were seen to have constituted the source imitated or borrowed from by all subsequent poets, were somehow group efforts, generated by a rich and rigorously conservative oral tradition that developed, refined, retained, and only imperceptibly innovated. To seek to define the contribution of any single bard, including those who gave their names to the traditions in question, became a meaningless undertaking, and the figure of Homer was replaced by "the *Iliad* poets" and "the *Odyssey* poets."

It is a commonplace of our own time that a committee cannot edit a text, much less create one. Language is intimate and refractory. Most of us harbor a conceptual model according to which, when we use language, we somehow impose form on matter, causing an artifact to take shape that is closely and necessarily bound up with our own perceptions of the world and our own sense of order. It is inevitably true that in order to imagine a tradition of oral epic composition we must set aside much of our own conception of what it means to use language, to generate an artifact of this sort, a poem or a narrative. What we are asked to believe is that a vast number of tiny contributions, over generations, can generate a product closely resembling one produced by the monumental synthetic effort of a single individual working for days, perhaps weeks or years, but in any case able to impose his will, his personality, on the final product and to make it his. A committee certainly could not create an *Iliad*, its last book subtly and ingeniously echoing the thematic organization of the first. But there are many sorts of collectives, and the comparison with a committee is misleading. My point is simply that those who categorically refuse the concept of a creative tradition rather than a creative individual as the author of the *Iliad* seem in general to base that refusal on a faith in the creative power of the individual—a manageable concept and the basis of virtually the whole of the subsequent tradition— combined with a reluctance to believe in the possibility of a collective art of such complexity and elegance. We should remember, though, that whatever the origin of the *Iliad* and *Odyssey*, they have served as the preeminent standard and model for subsequent European literary creativity. If the extreme "Parryist" model is sound, individual literary creation in the European tradition is thus the echo and the mimicking of the supreme preserved creation of a previous, collective tradition of storytelling. And if this is the case—and the individual act is shaped by mimicking and emulation of the collective act—we will be hard pressed to say where the limits of either mode of creativity lie.

If we have taken a rather long look at the ideological battle lines in the discussion of archaic Greek poetry today, it is because these matters impinge unavoidably on what we can say about Hesiod and the background of Hesiodic poetry. It should also be noted that in the discussion of Homer, the "anti-Parryists" are in the ascendant and the problem of orality has, with some justice, been thought to have occupied readers of Homer long enough. The more compelling problem, certainly, is to define in contemporary terms the special qualities of the distinctive voices tradition gives us as those of Homer and Hesiod. Nevertheless, the question of where these voices come from retains its fascination.

Parry himself was concerned for the most part with Homer and not Hesiod, and the same has been true of the majority of those who have pursued the implications of his discoveries. But if Homer has, for much of recent scholarship, been depersonalized and fragmented into "the *Iliad* poets" and "the *Odyssey* poets," the implications for Hesiod are clear. Or are they? Even those who emphasize the collective nature of what has been called "the Homeric encyclopedia" have in some instances wanted to see Hesiodic poetry as something derivative from the collective, traditional Homeric poetry, something secondary, marked by the imposition of an individual poetic identity and other earmarks of literate creativity. The similarities that link Homeric and Hesiodic poetry are, however, more striking than the differences.

Neither the *Iliad* nor the *Theogony* is written in a form of the Greek language actually spoken by any identifiable historical community of Greek speakers. Rather, this poetry was created in a composite epic diction, an artificial (or, more properly, "artistic") amalgam of regional dialects incorporating forms characteristic of the spoken language of a number of communities. Thus, words that would sound natural to a native of Lesbos ("Aeolisms") stand side by side with words characteristic of the spoken language of Ionia or of Athens, and even, occasionally, of Sparta. The language is international, transcending and incorporating local differences of dialect, just as the content draws on the traditions of various groups of Greek speakers to generate a common stock of heroic lore.

This mosaic of dialects does not jar with our understanding of Homeric epic. The anonymous, homeless Homeric voice speaks for many communities and retains forms and locutions characteristic of each. What is striking, though, is that in spite of its claims to Boeotian nationality, the Hesiodic voice expresses itself in the composite epic diction of the Homeric poems with the same preponderance of Ionic dialect. Although some apparently significant linguistic criteria allow us to make meaningful distinctions within the field of early Greek hexameter poetry, the language, the meter, the dialect, and even the store of formulas of the *Theogony* and the *Works and Days* are not strikingly different from those of the *Iliad* and the *Odyssey*. Those linguistic differences that can be measured seem to indicate principally that the Hesiodic poems evolved over a longer period than the Homeric.

A passage early in the *Theogony* provides an excellent example of the overlap and interaction between the Hesiodic and Homeric traditions. Complex arguments have been mustered to establish the precedence of Homer or Hesiod here— or, rather, to establish that Hesiod depends on the *Odyssey* or Homer on the *Theogony*. This pair of lines from the description of the good *basileus* (king) in the *Theogony* (91–92):

> *When he goes* through the court the people treat
>   him *as a god,*
> *with gentle reverence,   and he stands out among the*
>   *assembly,*

is largely the same as the last pair of this passage in the *Odyssey* (8.169–73):

> The other is a less handsome man,
> but a god crowns his words with elegance, and it is a
>   joy
> to look at him. He speaks without a fault,
> *with gentle reverence   and he stands out among the assembly,*
> *and when he goes* through the citadel the people look
>   on him *as a god.*

As we have seen, however, we are apparently dealing here with two parallel oral traditions that tap a common reservoir of formulas. The italicized phrases above are shared formulas, and those underlined are formulaic as well—that is, they are fixed expressions that occur elsewhere occupying the same position in the metrical pattern of the line. Eleven verses of the *Odyssey* open with the equivalent of the phrase *when he goes,* as do ten in the *Iliad.* More striking, though, the phrase *through the court* also occurs (though with a slightly different sense) in the *Iliad,* and the same is true of the phrase *the people treat him.* In other words, the Homeric tradition of song possessed all the fixed expressions the Hesiodic tradition uses in these two lines, and it is reasonable to assume that the absence of *through the citadel* and *the people look on him* in Hesiod is merely a question of the different subject matter and the much smaller bulk of the surviving Hesiodic corpus. The two traditions share a common reservoir of formulas and occasionally, as here, use them in ways that are so similar that one is tempted to say that the whole description—the aggregation of formulas, and not just the formulas themselves—is traditional. Yet to say that one imitates the other is meaningless, given the availability of the significant elements of the description in both the related traditions of song. One may be better than the other in the sense that to our taste the formulaic expressions seem more elegantly and appropriately joined in it. In this particular example, most would say that Hesiod wins the prize. But this is a situation in which excellence cannot be claimed to be a sign of priority (see Martin 1984).

The most striking difference between the two bodies of poetry is one of scale, and that difference is a very important one. Indeed, some of those who find a collective *Iliad* an absurd notion are nevertheless willing to concede that a poem like the *Works and Days*—or even more credibly the Hesiodic *Catalogue of Women*—might indeed be generated by a tradition of poets, over generations. The *Catalogue* is in fact a "string of beads," an apparently flexible assemblage of stock elements and figures, traditional motifs and narrative tropes, which can easily be imagined taking on a somewhat different form in each successive telling. The same can be said of large parts of the *Works and Days*, most obviously the agricultural advice, the wisdom poetry, and the *Days* themselves. The internal relationships of the elements of these passages and the relationships of the passages to each other seem largely arbitrary, and it does not stretch the imagination to attribute such compositional choices to the vagaries of improvisational performance, even for those who have little faith in the creative potential of such a mode of pre-literary creation.

Hesiod, then, is even more susceptible than Homer to reclassification as collective expression rather than original talent. But the coherence that "anti-Parryists" find in the "grand scheme" of the *Iliad* and the *Odyssey*—the thematic sophistication said to be the diagnostic mark of an individual talent—has its analogue in the autobiographical elements of the *Theogony* and the *Works and Days*. These are taken to guarantee a historical Hesiod just as the "grand scheme" guarantees a historical Homer, or at least these factors are said equally to point to the existence of a single creative talent in each tradition—and, given a single informing creative talent, no one will object to applying the traditional name, even if dates and biographical details elude us. The two bodies of evidence, though, are entirely disparate, and there is surely no reason to believe that the poems' claims about the identity of the speaker are any more to be trusted here than in the case of the much later *Anakreontea*. If literate poets could adopt the conventional persona of the drunken, erotic old man and speak as Anakreon, then surely their bardic predecessors could adopt the conventional persona of the shepherd of Mount Helikon and use it to berate the equally conventional idiot brother Perses, with no intent either to deceive or to mislead. Deception is an even less credible motivational model here than among the literate poets of the *Anakreontea*.

What is known of the conditions of performance of early Greek poetry lends some support to the idea that Hesiod and Perses were creations of a tradition of poetry rather than the reverse. First, singers and rhapsodes sang Hesiod as well as Homer. That is, competitions were held in which professional performers vied with one another in the recital of the poems of Hesiod—this much is clear from Plato's *Ion* (531). We can easily imagine the anonymous narrative voice of the *Iliad* in the mouth of a performer—the speaker could be anyone, and the performer easily slips into his place. Yet that performer would really make no less emphatic a claim to *be* Homer, or to give life to the voice of Homer, than a singer performing the *Theogony* or the *Works and Days* would make in impersonating Hesiod. In both instances we must imagine the performer identifying himself with the founder of the tradition. True, the Homeric narrative voice gives no autobiographical details, but its personal identity is strong, and that must have been felt in performance. Look at the second word of the *Odyssey*:

Tell me, Muse, about the man . . .

The performer who delivers that line is identifying himself, in the audience's mind, with the narrator, the poet—with Homer. The performer of the opening of the *Theogony* does not perform so different a task in adopting the persona of Hesiod, nor for that matter should the addition of the mechanism of a second (mute) persona, the addressee, Perses, be surprising, particularly in a poem like the *Works and Days* with its focus on the *relations* of men in society.

In both traditions, the Homeric and the Hesiodic, there was doubtless an initial creative stage, in which nonliterate, improvising singers manipulated and rearranged the traditional material, eventually developing it into something close to what we have—or, as some would claim, only remotely anticipating what we have and awaiting the "master poet" to give it final form. Next must have come the era of the noncreative rhapsode—Plato gives us his portrait in the *Ion*—who in a literate context and working from a fixed text transmitted and performed that text essentially unchanged. This last stage we can take to be historically documented, and Hesiod's "autobiographical" material was clearly at home in it. No doubt it was equally at home in the earlier, creative phase.

If it seems probable from our perspective that the Hesiod of the poems was a figure of convention rather than a historical individual, there is nevertheless little evidence that the ancients had any doubts about the matter. The biographical tradition, including the *Contest*, naturally insists on the historicity of its subject. As we shall see, however (chap. 5, below), certain elements of the Hesiodic persona were to have an afterlife as conventional trappings of Hellenistic and Augustan poetry. For Virgil and his contemporaries, the creator of the *Works and Days* was simply *Ascraeus*, the man of Askra. The implication is clearly that Hesiod's assertion that his father had come from Kyme

> and settled next to Helikon in a miserable village,
> Askra, bad in winter, awful in summer, and never any
> good
>
> [*W&D* 639–40]

was taken as confessional, an accurate description of a historical event. But the rest of the elements of the conventional picture of the shepherd poet that gained prominence in Hellenistic and Roman poetry have little to do with the picture of Hesiod woven by the biographers. The initiatory scene with the Muses and their laurel was evoked repeatedly, and its central figure came to stand for the activity of poetry in the broadest sense. We cannot of course know whether Kallimakhos and Virgil thought of this figure as a historical one, rooted in the experience of a genuine shepherd on Mount Helikon in the dim past (and subsequently elaborated to heroic stature, with an aura of divinity) or as a poetic fiction created to represent the sources of poetic fiction. The elements of the Hesiodic persona had in any case *become* conventional by the third century B.C., their connection to the life of any individual reduced to vestigial motifs.

As the example of the *Anakreontea* has shown, the tool of comparison can offer help in exploring the complex interaction of convention and experience in the poetry before us. Closer to Hesiod and often compared with him is the elegiac poet Theognis. A very substantial body of poetry—nearly 1400 lines—survives under this name and it has long been recognized that the identity of the poet is to be classified among the conventions of the genre. The Theognidean corpus embodies the ideology of an aristocratic group—probably that of Athens rather than Megara, though Theognis identifies himself as a Megarian (1.23). Its most striking characteristics are a rather repellent and self-satisfied snobbery and an enthusiasm for pederasty that, by comparison with Theognis's chilling elitist pronouncements, is at least attractive for its human warmth. Theognis speaks as the spokesman of a class, not as an individual, and the corpus undoubtedly grew up over a number of generations, perhaps extending from the seventh century into the fifth. The most important fact about this corpus from our point of view is the presence in Theognis's poetry of an addressee, Kyrnos, to whom the poet's advice is offered. The persistent repetition of his name is the most important and striking factor unifying this body of material. It may well be the "seal" of Theognidean authenticity mentioned by the poet (1.19) (see Ford 1985).

The relationship between Kyrnos and the speaker is curiously difficult to define. In antiquity, he seems to have been taken for Theognis's *eromenos* (beloved), a superficially likely assumption, and *The Suda* makes it explicit—but none of the specifically erotic poems is addressed to him by name, and the observations on the joys and sorrows of pederasty the poet shares with Kyrnos (2.1353–56) seem more properly addressed to a fellow *erastes* (lover, pederast), perhaps a fellow banqueter, than to an eromenos. The relationship, in any case, is left vague. Whoever Kyrnos is, he is willing to listen to a great deal of pompous preaching from Theognis, and he is probably somewhat younger than the speaker—at least Theognis seems to be married and to recommend marriage to Kyrnos (1.1225–26).

More than seventy-five poems are addressed to Kyrnos by poets speaking as Theognis, but it is extremely likely that the poets in question belonged to several different generations. Thus it is also very likely that Theognis's companion was—or became—a conventional figure, a mute persona, and if that is given, then Hesiod's addressee, who has no identity outside of formulas of address—*(mega) nepie Perse* (Perses, you (big) fool)—is very likely to belong in the same category. This is not to say that neither a Kyrnos nor a Perses ever existed. The conventional figures may well have their origin in life; if so, then the situation lies beyond our capacities to date or to say anything specific about. We witness it only when it has been transformed into poetry, and here again parallel evolution provides the best analogy. Hesiod and Perses developed as a function of a body of poetry with a traditional form and content. This tradition of poetry had an origin, certainly, and a poet named Hesiod with a dolt of a brother names Perses may have stood at that origin. Nevertheless, we must assume the poems as they reach us to have passed through many minds and many hands. The poems have evolved and with them the persona of the poet and that of his mute interlocutor, so that these are best thought of from our perspective as products, or perhaps strategies, of the poetry and neither as its source nor as a historical record of its creator.

The Hesiodic Landscape and the Hesiodic Persona

Let us begin the song from the Helikonian Muses—
theirs is the great and holy mountain of Helikon—
who dance on gentle feet around the violet spring

and the altar of the mighty son of Kronos.
They wash their tender skin in the Permessos
or Hippokrene, the Horse's Spring, or the holy
  Olmeios,
and then perform their dances on the highest ridge of
  Helikon.

. . . .

These are the ones who once taught Hesiod the
  beautiful song
as he tended his sheep under holy Helikon.

—*Theog.* 1–7, 22–23

Homer betrays neither his name nor his home. The anonymous and impersonal narrative voice is bereft of location in space as it is bereft of personal identity. Hesiod is just the opposite, insisting on the details of his biography and at the same time on the physical landscape in which he situates himself. The special relationship between this text and a specific Greek landscape is inseparable from the text itself, simply because the speaker relentlessly situates himself in the little village of Askra on the slopes of Mount Helikon. If Homer chooses to be heard as an anonymous voice from nowhere, Hesiod will not allow us to forget where he is speaking from, and for that reason we must stop a moment and examine the landscape as woven by the text and its relationship to the real world.

If we are correct in asserting that Hesiod's biographical details are to be regarded as conventional tropes of the text, then we must suspect that the same is true of geographical givens. Gregory Nagy, who has relentlessly pursued the implications of this theory of the development of the Hesiodic corpus, suggests that Askra and Kyme are elements of convention in the *Works and Days*, emblematic of Hesiod's father's emigration from a once-rich colonial city in Asia Minor *back* to the Greek mainland, an inversion of the tradition expressed in the widespread *ktisis* (foundation) poetry of which only traces survive (Nagy 1982, 63). In general terms this account has the ring of truth, with the important reservation that we have absolutely no indication that Kyme was ever ruined or impoverished in the archaic period or that Hesiod wanted it to serve as an emblem of the city ruined by *hybris*, the arrogance bred of success. On the contrary, Kyme seems to have been an exceptionally rich city, at least from the late sixth century down to Strabo's time, and Hesiod mentions only his father's poverty—the city's poverty need not be inferred. It seems therefore far more likely that the autobiographical excursus (*W&D* 630–40) is meant primarily to underline the irony of Hesiod's inheritance. His father was indeed a reverse colonist, but he moved in poverty from a *rich* Aeolian city to a miserably poor place, where he himself was at least moderately successful. The fruits of that success, though, have been preempted by Perses with the help of crooked local administrators, and Hesiod finds himself a poor man in a poor place, one of the "shepherds who sleep in the fields, losers, nothing but stomachs" of the Muses' speech in the *Theogony* (26).

As for Askra itself, most recent commentators have blamed the town's bad reputation on Hesiod. A topographer who visited the location that tradition identifies as Hesiod's village in May 1973 found it "a delightful site with as pleasant and refreshing a situation as a Greek city could have" (Wallace 1974, 8). This may effectively undermine Hesiod's claim that Askra was "*never* any good"—and of course most of Greece could be described as "delightful" in May—but I can report from personal experience that around the date of the heliacal rising of Sirius in July (in Hesiod's time it has been calculated

that this would have been the equivalent of July 19), when
the thistle blooms and the cicada drones, Askra at two in the
afternoon richly deserves the epithet "awful" (argaleos; W&D
640, see below, p. 127). It is incidentally true that Askra is a
terrible spot for astronomical observations in the Hesiodic
manner. The heliacal rising of Sirius, for example (the first
appearance of that star just far enough ahead of the sun to
be visible in the morning sky), would be missed for days because the entire eastern horizon is obscured even at dawn by
dense heat haze, doubtless aggravated by pollution today but
largely natural. The upper reaches of the valley of the Arkhontitsa (Hesiod's Permessos) really are exceptionally airless
and stifling at that time of year. If you are courageous enough
to make the trek up through the pass to the west (now with
a passable vehicle road), what you find is quite literally a small
summer colony of herdsmen with their families, living in the
open (agrauloi; Theog. 26) or, more specifically, in tents. They
camp out there all summer, where it is wooded and relatively
cool, the water is good, and the pasture on the high slopes
of the spur of Helikon, today called Zagaras, supports sheep
and even cattle at a time when the lowland pastures are
brown, dry, and intolerably hot, both at Panaghia and Neo-
khori, where the modern shepherds have their homes, and at
nearby Askra. Several hours' walk above their camp will bring
you to Cold Well (Kriopigadhi), identified, no doubt with
some justification, as Hesiod's Hippokrene, and to find the
well with its ancient masonry on top of this remote ridge, still
in use for watering the summering flocks, is indeed a moving
experience. Sadly, though, my own observation confirms that
of others with regard to the water of Hippokrene: though
abundant, it is hardly appetizing.

What has this Boeotian landscape to do with the "real"
Hesiod, the historical Hesiod? My own answer would be: in

all probability, very little. But at the same time the poetry itself insists on its relationship to this valley, and for over two millennia tradition has confirmed that relationship. The historical facts are elusive, but we can at least sketch out a plausible historical model for the localization of this body of archaic poetry in this landscape. I take it that the Hesiod appropriated by the shrine in the valley of the Arkhontitsa was once as homeless as Homer. The poems as we have them have been adapted to the landscape, or the landscape to them, but the relationship is not an essential one. Let us agree from the start that the description that we get from Hesiod, though it includes place names, which give it an air of great specificity, is largely dictated by convention. Of course, Hesiod's carping irony about his village is a function of his poetic persona and not of any specific location—hundreds of dusty little agricultural towns in Greece are hideously hot in July and chillingly damp, and even snowy, in January. Furthermore, the place-names Hesiod gives us cannot be located on a map with any great certainty. We can visit what we take to be Hesiod's Askra and be moved by Hesiod's Hippokrene, but at the same time we should be perfectly clear that these identifications themselves are largely matters of convention.

Nevertheless, the association of the valley of the Arkhontitsa with the Muses of Helikon can be shown on archaeological evidence to go back to the Hellenistic period, at the very least. Askra was apparently destroyed by nearby Thespiai sometime before the fourth century B.C., and it was the people of Thespiai, not Askra, who in the third and second centuries built an altar to the Muses and a stoa near the stream and embellished a theater on the nearby slopes of Helikon. The theater itself is a natural hollow that may well have been in use before the Hellenistic building program. Nevertheless, evidence for an earlier sanctuary in the valley, one going back to the classical and archaic periods, is lacking, though the valley was demonstrably inhabited from an early date. The sanctuary was still thriving down into the Roman period, until Constantine stole the statues of the Muses to grace his new capital at Constantinople (where they were later destroyed). An abundance of Christian chapels attested to the valley's enduring status as a holy place, but it is probably coincidence that their number seems to have been the same as that of the daughters of Memory. It is quite possible, of course, that there was a continuous cult of the Helikonian Muses in the valley of the Arkhontitsa—or perhaps higher up at some as yet unexcavated location on the slopes of Helikon—from the archaic period. Given the available evidence, however, and the great popularity of Hesiod in the Hellenistic period, it is safer to assume that the cult came to be at a relatively late date, and that the poems themselves form its basis. Other Hellenistic shrines proclaimed their real or factitious prehistoric roots through archaizing architecture—a Mycenaean relieving triangle in a Hellenistic building on Samothrace is a striking example. There it is quite possible that the vogue of the *Argonautika* of Apollonios of Rhodes brought some increase in attention to the sanctuary (where Jason was initiated, according to the poem) and that the Mycenaean doorway was intended to refer to the shrine's deep and holy past. The Valley of the Muses had no such archaizing architecture but may still represent a parallel development—a shrine intensely developed in the Hellenistic period but basing on literary evidence a claim to very early origins. The possession of a quadrennial festival of the performing arts—the Mouseia—on the exact spot of the cult of the Helikonian Muses proclaimed by Hesiod was doubtless a source of pride and revenue to Thespiai, and Hesiod's evidence fit the valley of the Arkhontitsa well enough.

The topography of Askra, Hippokrene, and the other Hesiodic sites is reasonably secure, then, from the Hellenistic period. Before the third century B.C., however, we have nothing but the traditions passed down by the poems and secondary traditions derived from these. It would be no great surprise to learn that Askra, whose name to a native speaker would mean "Barren Oak," is not to be found on any map and that the Hesiodic topography of western Boeotia was a decor created by the Theogony and the Works and Days rather than the one in which they themselves were created. We now know, since the work of the Cambridge-Bradford Boeotian Expedition in 1982, that there was in fact a large village on the slopes of the hill with the ruined tower that has been shown to tourists as the site of Askra from Pausanias's day to our own. This may have been Askra and in turn may have been Hesiod's home. But from the time of our first evidence for an association of Hesiod with this landscape, this village was only a ruin and a memory—one that lent dignity and authenticity to a Hellenistic festival and as such took on a life of its own.

Not all of the poems require every persona or site. Perses and Hesiod's father, to the best of our knowledge, had no existence outside of the Works and Days, and the same is true of Askra. Hesiod, as we have seen, is explicitly mentioned only in the Theogony, as is Hippokrene, though both poems mention Mount Helikon (a designation applied in modern times to the entire southeastern spur of the Parnassos massif, some forty kilometers in length and indented by many small valleys of which that of the Arkhontitsa is only one). The Shield of Herakles has no room for autobiography or any sort of dramatization of the speaker. Its narrative voice is every bit as anonymous as that of the Iliad. The same would appear to be true of the other works attributed to Hesiod. Of these the *Catalogue of Women* was read in antiquity as an adjunct to and extension of the *Theogony* (see below, pp. 45–48), and so the identification of the narrative voice as Hesiod's in the *Theogony* would carry over. If, as has been suggested, the entire *Theogony* is to be classified as an expanded prelude (analogous to one of the *Homeric Hymns*), a preface to a bardic performance, and it is therefore appropriate for the singer to assert his identity here and not elsewhere, then we would not expect to find Hesiod referring to himself in the other poems (Nagy 1982, 53). The little that we know of the eight poems that survive only in fragments does not contradict this suggestion.

In reviewing the data we have on the figure of Hesiod and Hesiodic topography, I have emphasized the weakness of our reasons for equating this information with historical and geographic truth. Finally, though, does it matter whether the poem was created by Hesiod or Hesiod by the poem? It matters very little, but what *is* important is that we are dealing here with a body of poetry whose relationship to tradition is strikingly different from that of subsequent poetry. Early Greek hexameter poetry became literature only secondarily. Before it could be written down it existed for an unknown period of time as a series of traditional motifs and stories— many of them with close parallels in other Indo-European and non-Indo-European traditions—passed down from generation to generation by performers ignorant of a fixed text who recreated the poem in every performance.

The poems of Hesiod represent the expression in writing of one—perhaps it would be better to say *several*—of those traditions of song. There are glimmerings of a perception of this special status in antiquity. The Jewish historian Josephus late in the first century after Christ observed that "they say [Homer] did not leave his poetry in writing, but it was transmitted by memory and later assembled from the songs, and that is why it contains many contradictions" (*Against Apion* 1.12). This passage attracted attention nearly two centuries ago, but it was not until our own that its full implications for the understanding of authorship in archaic Greek poetry were perceived. In the interim, two thousand years of tradition had affirmed that the shepherd of Askra was the author of the *Theogony* and the *Works and Days*. We are no longer in a position to say, "Hesiod was born in Askra in Boeotia about 750 B.C.," as if this were information on the order of "Wordsworth was born at Cockermouth, Cumberland, in 1770." Rather, we must perceive Hesiod as a mask for many anonymous voices, all trained, and trained well, over generations to sound the same, to speak with the same identity, and to pass on the same traditions. Given this model of the formation of the Hesiodic corpus, we may view in a new light Aelian's puzzlement over the problem of determining just which lines—indeed, which poems—were Hesiod's. Those who believe in a recoverable historical Hesiod—and this group includes some of the great experts on Hesiod of our time—continue to attempt to define an essential *Theogony* and an essential *Works and Days*. The great Prussian philologist Wilamowitz, who did more than any other individual to shape the modern discipline of classical philology during the decades before the First World War, even strove for an essential *Works* with the *Days* excluded as something alien. Great intelligence and tremendous sensitivity to the language of Hesiod have been focused on this problem, but the results (like the results of nineteenth-century attempts to define an essential *Iliad* and *Odyssey*) have been less than satisfying, and there is no consensus because there are no sound criteria for distinguishing among the voices that speak through the mask of

Hesiod. Hesiod contradicts and repeats himself because Hesiod is a composite that defies analysis, a tradition and not an individual voice.

And yet this text, like other texts, bears a tantalizing resemblance to spoken language, and as we read it and give it breath we turn it into spoken language. A speaker must of necessity be a human being—a person and a personality— and as we read and so perform the *Theogony* and the *Works and Days* we take our place in the succession of bards, trying as we do so to hear clearly and to realize the endlessly elusive voice of the first bard. As the Russian formalist critics realized early in this century, the mythified biography of the author is a part of the reader's experience of the text, a projection that invariably constitutes a formative element in that experience. We cannot simply shrug it off, but we *can*, at the same time we project and acknowledge that biography as a frame for the text, remember both that in the special case of early Greek poetry the author is a trope of the text in a very radical sense and that the relationship of that trope to any historical or geographical reality—indeed, to anything outside the strategies of the text itself—is likely to be so complex that any hope of reconstructing it may be misplaced.

The reading of Hesiod that follows is therefore unitarian in the sense that it takes the whole of the material that comes down to us under Hesiod's name as the given and treats that material as a unit, though of course a fragmented one. This unitarianism implies nothing about the origin and history of this material, least of all that it is in any sense the creation of a single imagination, and regards as futile the attempt to isolate the thought of any single individual in what is clearly a complex body of traditional material. One might as fruitfully ask precisely which verses of the Pentateuch are *really* the work of Moses.

Even if such an undertaking were feasible, the attempt to restore life and breath to a single performance in the history of the traditional material before us—the best performance, let us say, of "Hesiod" himself, wherever in the archaic history of the tradition we might put him—would be at best (as Hans-Georg Gadamer might say) an imitation of an imitation. Gadamer applies Plato's phrase specifically to the performance of early music on early instruments, emphasizing the fact that the work exists only as realized and that the attempt to recreate an earlier realization is a peculiar form of archaeology. Fascinating and tantalizingly attractive as such endeavors may be, they lie at one remove from the more immediate question of how to perform—that is, to read—this traditional material here and now, using the fullest resources of our own culture and searching to bring it to life in relation to ourselves.

II THE THEOGONY

Theogonies

THE PERSONA OF THE SHEPHERD POET, THE PEASANT, SO dominates the tradition's perception of the Hesiodic corpus that it is the *Works and Days* rather than the *Theogony* that has seemed the essential Hesiod. Even in antiquity, we have Pausanius's testimony that the *only* poem recognized as genuine by the priests in the valley of the Muses was the *Works and Days*:

> Those of the Boeotians who live around Helikon assert (following their tradition) that Hesiod wrote nothing but the *Works and Days*, and they even exclude the prologue [*prooimion*] to the Muses from that poem, claiming that the beginning is the part about the two strifes.
>
> [9.31.4]

Nevertheless, the *Theogony* has for modern readers moved to the central position, simply because it answers questions we find far more compelling than those addressed in the *Works and Days*. We have learned, since Vico, to see the myths of cultures remote in time and space as keys to understanding those cultures, and this has meant that texts that can be taken to offer canonical or authoritative versions of myths have taken on great importance.

The Hesiodic account of the origins of the gods (and,

incidentally, of the universe) was certainly influential and from our perspective represents a valuable norm against which to test other accounts—but it was far from authoritative. There are several reasons for this, most important among them the fact that the gods of the Greeks belonged first and foremost to art, not to cult. From the earliest glimpses we ⟵ have into Greek tradition, the poets and visual artists, not the priests, were the bearers of the traditions about the divine. The contrast with the priest-ridden cultures of the East has often been drawn but cannot be too much emphasized. The Greeks had no Moses, and their first theologians were entertainers—Homer and Hesiod.

Since they were the earliest accounts, the Homeric and Hesiodic theologies were of central importance, but they always had competitors, and the stories themselves, when all is said and done, *had* no authoritative forms. It is striking in this context that an ancient account of the first definitive edition of the text of Homer and perhaps Hesiod (an account known to Cicero and reflected in the marginal notes of ancient scholars) suggests that it was in the civic festivals of Athens in the time of Peisistratos and his sons (561–10) that a fixed text was first established. Whether historically accurate or not, the story suggests an important contrast between the flexibility of the poems while entirely the possession of the poets (when presumably they could be adapted to their immediate context and manipulated for aesthetic effect) and the rigidity of those same poems once institutionalized, frozen and shackled to the interests of political power. Institutions demand—indeed, impose—stability and are able to harness the power of even such unlikely sources as poetry. But the fact that the Greek stories about the gods are endlessly self-contradictory (and thus mutually complementary in their contradictions) is an indication that they were never definitively harnessed and canonized. It was not until eight centuries after Peisistratos, when the later pagan Platonists were doing battle with Christians who were armed with the powerful weapon of their own canon, that the necessities of war spurred a largely effective attempt to close and fix the canon of Greek theology—and by that time it no longer mattered.

What can we offer as a context for the Hesiodic *Theogony*? What can be compared with it? From the perspective of the fifth century, four traditions of hexameter poetry of august antiquity existed, and of these Herodotos (*Hist.* 2.53) tells us that in his opinion those of Homer and Hesiod were the oldest. It is striking that his comment is worded in such a way that we might suspect he had before him a Homeric *Theogony*, but we are probably on safer ground if we assume that he knew a Hesiodic and a Homeric corpus each resembling the ones that have come down to us—at least in broad outline. Herodotus's mention of "poets thought by some to be earlier than [Homer and Hesiod]" points clearly to Orpheus and Mousaios, and of these the Orphic tradition of poetry, at least, whose narrative persona was the bard of the expedition of the *Argo* a generation before the Trojan War, could boast an account of the origin of the gods formulated in a manner closely comparable with that of Hesiod.

A substantial body of poetry speaking through the mask of Orpheus survives, but the sources for it are for the most part quite late, and until twenty years ago it was possible to doubt the existence of a body of Orphic theogonic and cosmogonic poetry before the time of Plato. The situation changed in 1961 with the discovery of a papyrus—the first ever recovered from Greek soil—associated with a late-fourth-century B.C. tomb at Derveni in Macedonia (cf. Kirk, Raven, and Schofield 1983, 30–33). Since that discovery, we find ourselves in the paradoxical situation that the oldest surviving evidence for a Greek theogony no longer relates to the canonical Hesiodic one (the earliest papyri of which date from the first century B.C.) but to one attributed to Orpheus, eighteen hexameters of which, embedded in a matrix of allegorizing commentary, found their way into a funeral pyre at roughly the time of Alexander the Great and against all odds were preserved. The verses themselves can hardly have been composed at the time the commentary was written, and it seems reasonable (following scholars who have worked on the papyrus) to date the verses to the sixth century B.C. Most of the Derveni hexameters are otherwise unknown, but a few are shared with an Orphic hymn to Zeus known from other, much later, sources. This raises the possibility that more of the received "Orphic" poetry may have existed and gone under the name of Orpheus at an unexpectedly early date (though of course the conventional working assumption that our Hesiodic *Theogony* antedates all this material is not seriously threatened).

The Derveni theogony is too fragmentary to permit a detailed comparison with the Hesiodic *Theogony*. It appears, though, to involve a sequence of generations closely comparable to Hesiod's and a succession by castration. It may well be the case that the Derveni theogony had Zeus castrate his father, Kronos, as Kronos had castrated Ouranos in the canonical story—this is the situation at any rate in an Orphic cosmogony preserved by the Neoplatonist Porphyry. One of the most striking episodes of the Derveni cosmogony—and here we must take the commentator's word for the meaning of a lost portion of the text—has one of the gods in the succession swallow the severed genitals of his predecessor. It is probable that the commentator in fact misreads the text here, but this would not matter for our purposes. The meaning he finds in the text is at least as interesting as the fragmentary text itself. This grotesque scene, with its crude but unambiguous representation of the transfer of power, would be interesting in its own right, but its true significance comes out in comparison with other, more remote theogonies. The oldest preserved Indo-European succession myth—a Hittite text relating a Hurrian story, a millennium older than the Greek theogonies in the form known to us—contains the same motif. The god Kumarbi in this case bites off and swallows the genitals of his defeated predecessor, Anu, in the process becoming pregnant with the next generation of gods. This detail is of interest here because it points to the vastness of the stream of tradition tapped by Hesiod's *Theogony*. That stream probably sprang up in the fertile crescent at a time even before the differentiation of the Semitic languages and several millennia before the first evidence for Indo-European. It took various forms in different cultures from Sumer to Babylon, Ugarit, Boğazköy, and eventually Greece. By comparison with the theogonies that survive from other Near Eastern sources, the Greek manifestation of the theogony strikes us as civilized, refined, belated: a link between the rich creativity of the East and our own cultural heritage, which the Greeks did so much to shape. In this the Greek theogony is emblematic of the status of Greek art and literature in general when juxtaposed with their Eastern counterparts.

The detail of the swallowed genitals in the Derveni theogony—an element in the traditional Near Eastern succession myth foreign to the canonical Greek version and otherwise unknown in a Greek context—says a great deal about the editing process of the tradition of religion-as-poetry. The Derveni commentator is clearly displeased with the apparent meaning of the story he is discussing. He immediately (and no doubt correctly) explains it as an allegorical representation of the transfer of creative (generative) power, and he does the same thing with another noncanonical element in the theogony before him, an account of incest between Zeus and his mother. Neither motif became canonical—we would not even know they existed in Greek theology were it not for the chance preservation of the Derveni papyrus. They are representative, however, of a small but fascinating class of noncanonical motifs that link Greek religious thought to the East. Perhaps the most striking of these is the painting of Hera and Zeus performing fellatio, seen by the Stoic Khrysippos, perhaps at the great Heraion of Samos. Whatever the source of this image—and the episode was widely reported since it was dear to the hearts of muckraking Church Fathers eager to point out the depravity of pagan religion—it evokes the erotic theological art of India and strikes a shocking discord when we try to place it in the context of our own vision of an archaic Greek temple. My point is simply that Greek art, religion, and poetry as we know them are characterized by a certain style, a style perhaps best understood in terms of the *exclusion* of a vast range of possibilities rather than in terms of a specific internal creativity. The most nearly authoritative Greek theogony—Hesiod's *Theogony*—is a magnificent example of this. The latest in date of the great Near Eastern theogonies, it is likewise the most refined and the most coherent—though in the context of Greek poetry it nevertheless stands out for its primitive violence and fierceness. In terms of Near Eastern theological tradition and myth, it is belated, effete, reduced, and manipulated in such a way that, unlike its predecessors, it is accessible to us as a work of art, with the imaginative power and aesthetic focus that that status implies. In terms of Greek poetry, however, it is primitive, a rough lump of poetic matter barely differentiated from the chaotic mass of tradition that constitutes its source and its core.

There were, then, other Greek theogonies, and even the

closely related Homeric and Hesiodic traditions sometimes disagree about a god's pedigree. Beyond this authentically archaic core, the range of Greek theogonic imagination finds expression in a good deal of hexameter poetry—most of it Orphic—which develops versions of the origin of the gods and the world sometimes wildly at variance with Homer and Hesiod. This poetry is a patchwork of derivative elaborations and of authentically archaic, traditional material. In no instance can the lines of transmission be satisfactorily shown, but the whole mass of this poetic theogonic speculation is, finally, the characteristically elegant Greek manifestation of the same cultural tradition that elsewhere produced the rough generations of Kumarbi and Anu, no less than those of El and Ba'al.

The Shape of Our Theogony

Since the other Near Eastern theogonies, including the Greek rivals of Homer and Hesiod, reach us only in fragmentary form, we have little to compare with Hesiod's poem and little basis for a description of how and why early Greek poetry approached the subject of the origins and relationships of the gods. We have a rudimentary description of a cosmogony placed in the mouth of Orpheus in the *Argonautika* of Apollonios (1.496–511), a short but quite Hesiodic-sounding theogony likewise sung by Orpheus in the "Orphic" *Argonautika* (419–31), and a brief suggestion of a theogony in the Homeric *Hymn to Hermes* (54–61).

The latter example—the only one preserved in an archaic poem—may support the idea that the genealogies of the gods were proper matter for prologues, or *prooimia* (Nagy 1982, 53), but the evidence is slim at best. Prologues of this sort would appear to have served regularly as introductory pieces in performances of heroic poetry. The collection of hymns to the gods that comes down to us under the name of Homer is an anthology of prologues, though the longest of these must have been unwieldy for such use. The entire *Theogony* seems to have served as prooimion to the *Catalogue of Women*, but it is more than twice the length of the longest of the Homeric *Hymns*, and if the anthology of the *Hymns* throws any light on the *Theogony*, we can only use it to conclude that the *Theogony* is a very overloaded prooimion, one so expanded as to develop a complex internal structure of its own at the cost of its usefulness as a practical introductory piece. We are not compelled to interpret the evidence in this way, but it provides a credible and attractive account of at least one stage in the formal development of this traditional material.

If indeed the *Theogony* is a sort of Brobdingnagian prooimion, then its first and most striking formal peculiarity is that it has developed internally its *own* prooimion, itself longer than all but a few of the Homeric *Hymns*. The status of this prooimion (*Theog.* 1–115), like that of the much shorter one of the *Works and Days* (1–10), has been problematic since antiquity. Both were rejected by the Pergamene scholar Krates, and that of the *Works and Days* was likewise condemned by the Alexandrian Aristarkhos. Krates' comment on the matter seems to be preserved by a Byzantine commentator in a general discussion of prooimia: "Those of Hesiod's *Works and Days* and *Theogony* could be put in front of any poem. That is why Krates legitimately athetized [that is, rejected] them." Assuming that this was in fact Krates' opinion, *and* assuming that the *Theogony* prooimion as transmitted was the one he had in front of him, his literary judgment is certainly called in doubt here. There may be few champions of the 10-line prooimion of the *Works and Days*, which in any case was absent from certain known ancient copies of the poem, but the

115-line hymn with which our *Theogony* opens is in fact highly adapted to the poem it introduces, and numerous studies have shown that it is quite successful in giving us what the aforementioned commentator demands of prooimia: "the demonstration of the matters [the poet] will speak of, and what the subject and the whole purpose of the treatise are."

This somewhat surprising ancient literary judgment brings up several problems. First, why do we have a *Theogony* and a *Works and Days* transmitted with inseparable prooimia (in spite of respectable Hellenistic philological opinion), while the *Iliad* and *Odyssey* are delivered to us without prooimia but with a separate anthology of introductory pieces (the Homeric *Hymns*) attributed to the same author? Most attempts to answer this question have been based on distinctions of genre, but we simply do not have enough surviving major hexameter poems to be able to say that certain types (including wisdom poetry) were considered inseparable from their prooimia, while others (including heroic epic) were not.

A possible solution to this dilemma emerges if we try reading the two poems *without* their respective prooimia and ask ourselves what we have lost. The most conspicuous losses are the Muses, who, once the prooimia are removed, shrink to the status of Homer's Muses. That is, they are routinely invoked to aid in the execution of exceptional feats of memory and song, nothing more. Without the prooimia we no longer have a Hesiod with a special devotion to the Muses. We must not ignore the passage in the *Works and Days* (656ff.) where the speaker claims to have dedicated a tripod to the Helikonian Muses and to have learned song from them on Mount Helikon—but this passage has long been seen as an *aition*, or explanation, for an artifact actually displayed at the festival on Helikon, and as such it is suspect. This is not to say that it is "later" than the "rest" of the poem, since as we have seen the poem has no definitive form. To make this sort of claim credible, we would have to be able to answer the question "Later than *what*?" and we cannot. Suffice it that Hesiod's special devotion to the Helikonian Muses is supported only in the prooimion of the *Theogony* and in a passage in the *Works and Days* where explicit reference is made to the cult site that was the home of their festival.

We should also say that, reading the poems without their prooimia, in a sense we no longer have a Hesiod at all, since the narrative voice names itself only once and only here (*Theog.* 22). And along with Hesiod's name we lose every Boeotian toponym except Askra and Helikon, which occur together in the passage in the *Works and Days* where the tripod is explained. Gone are the eddying Permessos (which we identify with the Arkhontitsa), gone are holy Olmeios, Hippokrene, and the altar of Zeus on Helikon. The Hesiodic landscape is left impoverished and nearly anonymous, and the poet himself without a name. To put it differently, without the prooimia, Hesiod approaches the condition of Homer.

What is striking, then, is the way in which certain types of information cluster around the autobiographical data provided by the speaker. When Hesiod refers to himself, he almost invariably refers to the Boeotian landscape and to the Muses. And if we turn the problem around and remove the passages in question, we find we have lost Boeotia and the Muses along with Hesiod.

The status of the prooimia is crucial here, because the heart of the autobiographical, topographic, and Muse-cult material is found in the prooimion of the *Theogony*. My own suspicion is that the transmission of prooimia, and of these particular prooimia, in the received text of our *Theogony* and *Works and Days* is a function of the *idea* of Hesiod that was current at the time when we can first credibly maintain that

written copies proliferated—the Hellenistic period. We know
that the festival of the Muses in the valley of the Arkhontitsa
near Thespiai had by that time institutionalized the poems
and the persona of their singer. Once that had happened and
a powerful institution was constantly reminding the Hellenistic reading public of the association of Hesiod, the Muses,
and the slopes of Helikon above the Arkhontitsa, there could
no longer be any question (*pace* Krates) of putting the opening
invocations to the Muses aside as material not integral to the
poems. This is not to say that the prooimia are Hellenistic
forgeries. When and how they became associated with the
rest of the material are questions no longer susceptible to
meaningful inquiry. But it is highly probable that the institution of the Mouseia of Thespiai was the catalyst that guaranteed the transmission of the *sort* of Hesiod we have, a
confessional, self-referential Hesiod who situates himself in a
specific landscape and celebrates the Muses in a way otherwise unknown in archaic Greek poetry.

The prooimion of the *Theogony* is followed by an account
of the beginnings of reality that is as abrupt as it is sublime.
The genealogical model that will be the main organizing principle of the *Theogony* is already present in the prooimion,
which starts from the proposition:

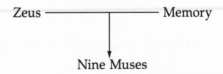

That this is something other than a historical narrative is
clear from the start. What this poetry does is to elaborate on
relationships among entities fundamental to our experience,
entities such as art, memory, power, and love. The building

blocks of the human universe are to be set in order, and the
principal tool at the disposal of this tradition of song for ex-
pressing such relationships is genealogy. The very first entities simply spring into being, divorced from any source or
mechanism of generation:

First of all, then, Khaos came to be . . .

[116]

But subsequently the genealogical model in the form "$A + B$
gave birth to C" is dominant.

The further implications of this genealogical model will
be explored later. Our purpose here is to look at the poem as
a whole, define its parts and their relationships, and draw
what conclusions we can from such an overview.

453–506 Kronos + Rhea: Zeus, Hestia, Demeter,
         Hera, Hades, Poseidon
507–616 Iapetos + Klymene: 4 children = the re-
         bellious Titans, including
    535–616 Prometheus, whose story includes
        570–616 Pandora
617–885 The Battle of Zeus against the Titans
    820–80 Typhoeus
    881–85 End of the war—Zeus distributes the
           honors of the gods
886–1018 Offspring of the Olympians
    886–929 The wives and children of Zeus
    930–62 Various matings of first- and second-gen-
            eration Olympians
    963–1018 Offspring of goddesses who married mor-
             tals
1019–22 Transition to *Catalogue of Women*

The arbitrary nature of this graphic outline, with its imposed subordination of passage to passage, must be kept in
mind. The organization of the whole is in fact accumulative
and characterized by parataxis, or juxtaposition, rather than
subordination. It proceeds by juxtapositions and elaborations
that depart from some element in the text and may or may
not return to their point of origin. When such a development
does proceed in a self-contained, orderly way, returning to its
original point of departure, it is said to show "ring composition," a pattern characteristic of oral composition but not
prominent in the *Theogony*.

As the name implies, ring composition designates a narrative pattern in which the speaker returns to his point of
departure. Moreover he returns by the same route he took in
embarking on the tale, coming back to the same ideas or mo-

tifs in reverse order. The resultant pattern is somewhat analogous to the arrangement of musical themes in classical
sonata form: *A–B* . . . *B–A*. In the absence of highly developed
Hesiodic examples, we may take as typical the passage in the
Iliad (24.599–620) where Akhilleus is speaking to Priam, come
to reclaim the corpse of Hektor, and evokes the story of the
mourning Niobe. The speech develops as follows (reading
clockwise from the top):

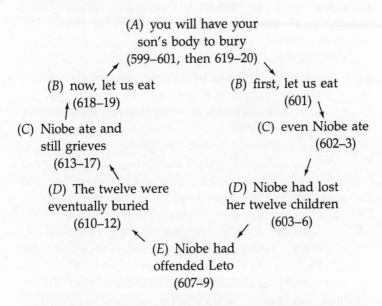

(A) you will have your
son's body to bury
(599–601, then 619–20)

(B) now, let us eat
(618–19)

(B) first, let us eat
(601)

(C) Niobe ate and
still grieves
(613–17)

(C) even Niobe ate
(602–3)

(D) The twelve were
eventually buried
(610–12)

(D) Niobe had lost
her twelve children
(603–6)

(E) Niobe had
offended Leto
(607–9)

M. L. West singles out six rings in the *Theogony* (37–52,
53–62, 411–15 with 426–49, 629–36, and 713–819). Most are
short passages that might be qualified as digressions and that
close with strong echoes of sound and sense, sometimes in
the form of a repeated line. The most substantial example,
the great ring in the titanomachy (713–819), has a clearly defined *A–B* . . . *B–A* structure framing a development of about

a hundred lines. There are, however, many better examples of ring composition in Homer than in Hesiod, doubtless because the technique serves primarily for episodic digression from linear narrative, of which there is relatively little in Hesiod. Rings are also found with significant frequency in the speeches that are so prominent a part of the Homeric corpus, and as a result it has been suggested that they reflect the mnemonic techniques of the preliterate rhetor as well as the preliterate bard. But Hesiod's characters do not deliver speeches as Homer's do, and this larger stylistic difference is reflected in the relative paucity of ring composition in Hesiod.

Still, if the poem itself is most obviously characterized by the compositional principles of juxtaposition and elaboration, when we stand back from it we may nevertheless perceive large units within it. The most clearly defined of these is the prooimion, but the remainder of the poem seems to break down naturally into (1) the account of the first beings and their offspring, followed by (2) the offspring of the Titans, and finally (3) the offspring of the Olympians. This last section is the least orderly and the most problematical for those concerned with isolating the "original" poem. West, here the most extreme of the lot, would end the *Theogony* at line 900, but he offers a catalog of the more conservative estimates (West 1966, 398). The problem is that the poem as we have it contains a bridge passage that once linked it to the *Catalogue of Women*, now preserved only in fragmentary form. Discussion of the latter part of the poem has usually centered on the question *where* the "true" *Theogony* ends and the material adapted to the introduction of the *Catalogue* begins. If the *Catalogue* were preserved intact, we might indeed be forced to read the *Theogony* as an enormously elaborated prooimion to that poem. Even in its absence, we are unable to postulate an integral *Theogony* as if its association with the *Catalogue* were something demonstrably belated, the adaptation of a genuinely archaic poem to a "later" one. In fact, when the *Theogony* and the fragments of the *Catalogue* are submitted to advanced stylistic and linguistic analysis, it is the *Catalogue* that appears less "advanced" and therefore presumably somewhat earlier in date than the *Theogony*.

If parts of the final section have been thought of as extraneous to the *Theogony*, the same is true of the earlier sections, and here agreement on which portions are "authentic" is an even more remote goal. Certain passages stand out as exceptionally rich and independent elaborations and sometimes show apparently significant linguistic deviation from their contexts. Most important among these is the Hekate episode (411–52), which seems out of proportion to the treatment of other comparable deities (cf. West 1966, 276–80), and the Typhoeus episode (820–80), containing the most baroque and audacious language in the corpus, comparable only to that of the *Shield of Herakles*. The Typhoeus episode has had few defenders except West (1966, 379–83), whose discussion of the problem is testimony to his excellent sense of the range of possibilities open to the Hesiodic diction. In defending the passage, he develops resemblances to the seafaring episode of the *Works and Days* (618ff.), which, as we have seen, is the single passage outside the prooimia that suggests an intimate association between the speaker and the Helikonian Muses, at the same time providing an aition for an object displayed by their priests. It is probable that the two rather aberrant passages belong to the same level of the development of the Hesiodic corpus, a level characterized both by Aeolic dialect forms and by a certain stylistic and imaginative outrageousness. But to say on this evidence that they are not integral to the corpus, or that we can distinguish here and only here the work of an individual and idiosyncratic poet, would be to

make claims about the creativity of individual Hesiodic singers that we cannot substantiate. Of course, the *Works and Days* passage, simply because it claims to be autobiographical, has by most critics (with the significant exception of Plutarch; see pp. 131–32 below) been taken to be authentic. We can no longer take that reasoning seriously, but neither can we turn around and eject both passages from a corpus whose development appears vastly too complex to be divided credibly into individual oeuvres.

We have, then, a prooimion and three major movements, each composed of smaller elements that vary significantly in importance among themselves. This tripartite schema shapes the poem as we perceive it, as analytic readers, though it would be pretentious to claim that it belongs inherently to the work. What does appear essential to the poem on the level of compositional principles is the genealogical model, first of all, and then a remarkably open-ended process of juxtaposition and elaboration, sometimes along the lines of ring composition.

The Prooimion

We have already noted the oddity that the poems of Hesiod come down to us with inseparable prologues, or prooimia, and it has been suggested that these prooimia serve to a very considerable extent to give the Hesiodic corpus and its singer their individuality. Let us look now at this extraordinary hymn to the Muses in context. The opening 115 lines of the *Theogony* constitute the essential self-portrait of the tradition, the account of the origins of Hesiodic wisdom poetry integrated into the poem itself. If the Homeric corpus tells us that Homeric praise poetry was sung by the bronze-age heroes in the field (*Il.* 9.189) and by bards at the feasts of the

bronze-age nobility (*Od.* 1.325–59, 4.17–18, 8.487–520, and so on), the parallel ancestor portrait delivered by the Hesiodic singers must be sought here. It is a vastly richer and more detailed portrait than the composite Homeric one, insisting as emphatically on the personality and specificity of the creator of its tradition as the Homeric tradition insists on the amorphous and collective nature of its own origins. As the first developed, personal portrait of the artist in the tradition of European poetry, it is certainly the most influential and the most imitated passage in the Hesiodic corpus. What it relates is the invention of a certain kind of poetry, but as an account of the invention of the poet it provided a template for subsequent accounts of the activity of poetry.

The prooimion is really two poems. The first (1–36) contains all the autobiographical material and serves as an introduction to—and a claim of special authority to sing—the second (37–115), a hymn to the Muses incorporating a thematic outline, a table of contents so to speak, of the *Theogony* proper and concluding with an invocation (104–15).

The pro-prooimion, as we may designate the first part, has an extraordinarily richly wrought poetic surface, and so resembles the short prooimion of the *Works and Days*. Place-names cluster densely in the opening lines, and it is difficult to believe that what is described here is not the valley of the Arkhontitsa, the site of the Boeotian festival of the Muses. The voice begins with the Muses, elaborates a highly determined landscape around them, and then describes their song and its contents, a description that turns out to be a capsule summary of the *Theogony* itself. But in fact at least three outlines of theogonies here succeed one another, subtly modulating the emphasis and order of their elements. The first, the evocation of the Muses' song (9–21), starts from Zeus and Hera and lists the major Olympians in a colorful rush of

names and epithets that reverses the sequence of genealogical
priority to reach Gaia, Okeanos, and finally Night (as if the
blackness of nonbeing were the true source and the foil for
the brilliance of these primal beings). The recapitulation (43–
52) *starts* from the idea of a divine succession (*theon genos*),
beginning as the first statement had ended, and derives this
succession from Gaia and Ouranos, but now the entire song
is situated in the house of Zeus and designates him and his
power as its second focus, followed by the *genos*, lowest in
prestige and priority, of men and giants. Zeus, then, is already
presented here as the container, the condition of all that is
said, and at the same time as a mediator, the entity standing
between the genos of gods and that of men and giants. The
invocation that closes the prooimion (104–15) restates this sequential pattern, calling on the Muses to start with Gaia, Ouranos, Night, and Sea and to generate what is to be
simultaneously a cosmogony and a theogony, taking as pretext for the entire undertaking the question, "What of these
things came *first*?" These multiple juxtapositions of the same
elements constitute a characteristically Hesiodic organization.
Sequence manifests priority, but the voice slips easily from
one perspective to another, suggesting from the start that the
causes are always functions of their effects and that the final
effect is things-as-they-are, the conditions of our own being.

If Zeus has been seen from the multiple perspectives
adopted in the prooimion as source, culmination, and mediator in the sequence of classes of beings, another figure is cast
as mediator here in another, more clearly defined, sense—
Hesiod himself. After the initial evocation of the Muses' song,
the speaker reaches back over a substantial gap of ten lines
to put the Muses and their intervening song in relation to one
Hesiodos and to establish the claim that the Muses taught him
to sing. The name itself seems to be a generic description of

the speaker and etymologically to mean "he who emits the voice" (Nagy 1982, 49; cf. Nagy 1979, 296–97).

What exactly does it mean that Hesiod's name—the name by which the singer of this poetry designates himself— is susceptible to analysis into a phrase that is manifestly descriptive of the singer and his function? One possibility, of course, is that this was simply the man's name—attached as fortuitously to this historic individual as the name Wordsworth (surely an equally suspect epithet) was bestowed on the infant author-to-be of *The Prelude*. This is rendered unlikely, though not perhaps impossible, by the fact that no other Hesiods are mentioned in the preserved Greek literature and inscriptions. Furthermore, Hesiod is not unique among Greek poets in having a meaningful name. It must surely be an even greater coincidence than those just evoked if Stesikhoros (He-who-establishes-the-chorus) was simply the name of the paternal grandfather of the famous sixth-century choral poet and so was passed on to this grandson in the traditional Greek manner. In this instance, even the Byzantine lexica seem to reflect an understanding that the received name of this poet was an honorific title rather than a personal name. A further possibility, with more interesting implications, is that the name is indeed generic, its encoded but accessible meaning pointing back to the tradition that generated it. For the persona of a tradition of wisdom poetry from the depths of the Indo-European tradition to designate itself as the bearer or thrower of the voice is eminently credible. But we are left with a question: Which audiences of this poetry would have heard and perceived that level of meaning? There seems no doubt that it is woven into the poetry of the prooimion, where Hesiodos is juxtaposed with the Muses, themselves "projecting the (beautiful) voice"—(*perikallea*) *os-san hieisai* (10; cf. 43, 65, 67)—and echoes of sound and sublexical sense link singer and dictating inspiration together. But even if this is the genesis of the name, it would seem that the loss of the perception of Hesiodos as anything but an opaque or semiopaque proper name must have been a stage in the appropriation of the poems and their speaker to the purposes of the Mouseia of Thespiai, if indeed we are correct in supposing that that institution played a role in the final definition of the persona.

The Muses teach "the beautiful song" to Hesiod the shepherd of Helikon. The initiation is narrated in a very few lines but falls neatly into a series of elements: (1) insults, (2) boasts, (3) gifts, and (4) commands. Why should the Muses begin by insulting Hesiod and his fellow shepherds? On a stylistic level, the answer is easy to find. The Hesiodic diction loves the unexpected, loves dramatic contrasts and foiled anticipations. The result is often at least implicitly humorous, as it is here. We have heard the beauty of the Muses' song praised repeatedly. We have been given a sample of that song in paraphrase, a glittering list of names of deities with rich epithets, ingeniously woven into a metrical whole that balances one against another. When the Muses finally open their mouths, the effect is unavoidably bathetic:

> Shepherds who sleep in the field, losers, nothing but
>   stomachs—
> we know how to tell lots of lies that resemble truth,
> and when we want to, we can sing authentic things.
>   [*Theog.* 26–28]

Again the mediating function comes to the fore, and the lower term of the relationship is defined with a clarity that is both comic and brutal. These coy—even arch—messengers stand between truth and the human condition. The latter is a state characterized by failure: the world's failure to satisfy the hungry gut and our failure to make it do so. This Boeotian hillside is a spiritual landscape whose apparent heirs in the tradition are the plain of La Mancha and the anonymous wasteland in which Samuel Beckett's marginal tragicomic figures pursue the implications of their humanity. The divine messengers have us at their mercy, and any attempt to see beyond the inadequacy of the world, to perceive anything but the hungry gut, is an act of faith dependent on an act of grace. Meanwhile, the bearers of grace undermine and destroy their own credibility.

But *why* do they call themselves liars? Of a number of traditional explanations perhaps the most frequently reiterated is the claim that these Muses want to discredit heroic (Homeric) epic as "lies that resemble truth" while exalting the rival Hesiodic wisdom poetry as the "authentic" article. This is a neat, pat, allegorical reading, and its implications are interesting. Still, I find it difficult to believe that these rival siblings—the Homeric and the Hesiodic traditions—should be reduced to this sort of explicit name-calling. Their rivalry is worked out at a far deeper level, and each knows itself and its rival for a combination of both truth and lies. Hesiod's Muses, after all, never suggest that they *will* tell Hesiod the truth or tell the truth through him. They simply point out that they *could*, if they wanted to. If their contradictory self-portrait leaves us with anything of substance, it is a characteristically evasive definition of art as a play of poses, a complex and implicating system of representation that constantly tantalizes us with the possibility that it represents *something*.

The Muses' gift to Hesiod is double. First, there is the staff, or scepter (*skeptron*, 30), a laurel branch that they cut for him, and then there is the "magic voice" (*thespin auden*, 31–32) that they inspire in him, perhaps as a function of the first gift. The immediate effect of these gifts is that Hesiod takes on the characteristics of the Homeric seers and sirens: he can tell the future and the past. His mind can travel freely in time and space, and his words can communicate what his mind perceives. His voice becomes one with the Muses' voice, and he becomes the evasive instrument of their imperfect mediation between truth and the wretched human condition. Why laurel? Odd as it seems, the scholiasts and Proklos (see above, pp. 4–5) take it as self-evident that Hesiod *ate* the laurel leaves and that the experience conveyed is one of chemically induced hallucinogenic "inspiration." Proklos, offended by this apparent meaning, goes on to allegorize and so spiritualize the passage, denying that it is a matter of mere physical intoxication—an effort of interpretation precisely paralleled in the Hindu interpretive tradition that denies that the Vedic *soma* was a hallucinogen and treats it as a symbol of a purely spiritual experience. The prophetic ecstasies of the Pythian priestess at Delphi were associated with laurel from the earliest information we have about the sanctuary, and it was claimed in late antiquity—perhaps earlier as well—that the smoke of burning laurel induced her visions, but though the plant is toxic I know of no real evidence that it is intoxicating. It would nevertheless seem that from the mid-fifth century at the latest—the scholiast quotes Sophokles—it was a commonplace that the eating of laurel was psychotropic, and we may conclude that the classical period must have understood the gift of the Muses to Hesiod in these terms.

Despite its long history, though, this odd explanation of Hesiod's laurel is reductionist and misleading in its attempt to restrict the symbol to a single sense, a single level of reference. This tradition of poetry is unlikely to have been the first to associate itself with laurel, the plant that belongs to Apollo as leader of the Muses (cf. 94–95). In fact, Apollo, the Muses and the activity of poetry, and the Pythia and the activity of prophecy are all intimately associated with laurel in ways that make the search for more specific elucidation of the symbol unnecessary. Whether the connection began with a drug-induced ecstasy or simply with the occurrence of abundant laurel at a site associated with Apollo (much as Athena doubtless became associated with the owl because owls conspicuously frequented her citadel), it was this nexus of associations, not its obscure origin, that gave the symbol its power.

The gifts delivered and Hesiod's consecration effected, the Muses instruct him to sing the genos of the gods and always to frame the song with opening and closing addresses to themselves. At this point occurs what is no doubt the strangest of the many transitions within the Hesiodic corpus. The narrative of the apparition of the Muses closes with the line:

> But what do I have to do with this business about an
> oak or a rock?
>
> [35]

And then the poem begins again from the beginning with a sort of rustic echo of line 1:

> You, then—let's start with the Muses . . .
>
> [36]

What, indeed, does the singer of a theogony have to do with the rustic landscape of bucolic poetry and with tales of shepherds on hillsides? The reference to oaks and rocks is not simply an evocation of that landscape, either, but a reference to a proverb also twice alluded to in Homer and explained in various ways by the scholiasts. Though neither the poetic uses of the proverb nor the explanations are entirely consistent, it seems clear that "oak and rock" are traditional places of discovery of babies—real or feigned foundlings—and that to trace one's ancestry to an oak or a rock is to invoke a colorful euphemism to account for one's lack of pedigree. So we have here an evocation of an old wives' tale—a conventional and even hackneyed account of things—but more, an old wives' tale that gives a fictional account of parentage, of birth and origin. What the narrative voice seems to be doing here is really something quite surprising: it is dropping its mask, its shepherd's pose, *and calling attention to it.* Hesiod is *telling* us that he is only playing at being Hesiod the shepherd of Helikon. The role is an elegant convention, one that has served to introduce the poem and to legitimize the voice of the singer—but it is not really the mask for the poet of a theogony, and it is set aside at line 35, never to be assumed again. The procedure is familiar enough in comedy—including Attic Old Comedy—where performers pass freely in and out of character, calling attention to the power of the artifice and doing so for comic effect. A similar procedure is clearly within the range of convention that shapes Hesiodic poetry, and this is among the most striking and telling differences between this tradition and the Homeric. More than his anonymity, it is the static uniformity of the Homeric speaker that distinguishes him from the Hesiodic voice. The latter not only has more detail in his persona, he has a variety of personas, modes, styles, and identities, and he draws attention to this variety— the poses themselves are problematized, woven into the rich surface of the poem with its elusive claims to tell the truth . . . if and when it chooses.

If this seems at first sight an idiosyncratic reading, it is at any rate not a new one. Several scholia on the passage indicate that this verse was read in antiquity much as I have explained it. Here is a representative sample of the sort of paraphrase of this passage we find in the marginal notes of the manuscripts:

> As if what he had started to say seemed inappropriate to him ("The Muses granted me . . ." etc.), and he says, "What does this sort of discourse have to do with me—oaks and rocks? What need do I have to adopt an old-fashioned style (*arkhaiologein*)? Poetry is mythology that resembles truth."

At the end of the pro-prooimion, then, as the scholiast acknowledges, Hesiod explodes his own myth, throws down the shepherd's mask, and exposes that persona for what it is—a charming poetic convention of an old-fashioned sort, a fairy tale.

The rest of the prooimion, beyond this odd abortive start, is a hymn to the Muses, incorporating passages that further define the singer's relationship to his audience and beginning with the second summary mentioned above. The song will be, first of all, that of Gaia and Ouranos, then that of Zeus, and finally will extend to the genos of men and giants. The first real application of the generative model, though, will be the account of the Muses themselves, a passage in which most readers have felt Hesiod was improvising creatively in a manner inconsistent with the straightforward transmission of a traditional theogony. While it is impossible to know just how much of this material is a function of the poem before us, it is nevertheless clear that the names of the Muses (77–79) are closely bound to the text from which they emerge and echo qualities already attributed to the group ("Famous," "Flourishing," "Lovely," "Heavenly") as well as activities in which they have already been described "She-who-delights-in-dance"). These embodiments of the arts seem to be taking shape and identity before our eyes—as if Homer and Hesiod really *were* the creative theologians Herodotos seemed to tell us they were, making up gods and attributes out of whole cloth. The Muses' genealogy is transparent allegory. Offspring of power and memory, they embody the prestige and authority of the highest of the gods, just as they stand for the entertainments that make the life of Olympus one of uninterrupted bliss.

The function of memory here is more difficult to define. It is little help to observe that the oral poet needed a good memory—I doubt seriously that what we usually designate as "memory" has much to do with the matter. Memory, in this context, is not the capacity eroded by Alzheimer's or obliterated by Korsakov's syndrome but rather a fine-tuned programming in a vast range of cultural skills and information. Memory is of course retrospective, and the implication is unavoidable here that the true models, patterns, and formulations lie in the past, to be recovered and *re*created in the present. To this extent, William Blake's attack on the limitations of the daughters of Memory (see below, p. 157) is relevant to the Hesiodic form of the story. But aside from Hesiod's association of Memory with Eleutherai (the town on Kithairon, we assume, perhaps rashly), we have no evidence for cults of personified memory. None, that is, but the Mnemosyne that is the opposite of Lethe in the "Orphic" gold tablets and related material—the closest thing we have to a Greek "book of the dead" offering instructions to the soul of the deceased on the best course of action in the other world. There, Memory is (or perhaps simply presides over) the spring that satisfies the thirst of those destined to be freed from the round of reincarnation. It is the initiation into true being, as opposed to the muddle of errors and pain that is this world. With characteristic precious wordplay, Hesiod identifies his Memory (*mnemosyne*) with forgetfulness (*lesmosyne*, 55) of suffering. Her gifts, then, constitute an alternative to the world, a sustaining vision of liberation from the existence we know. In a peculiar way, Hesiod's Muses are *less* the daughters of mere memory than Homer's. The function of the Muse of heroic epic is limited to the retrospective recall of information about the heroic past. Hesiod's are more ambitious and in a sense are on the way to becoming the daughters of inspiration Blake invoked to replace them.

The second account of the Muses locates them not in Boeotia but in Pieria, on the northern slopes of Mount Olympos, and in this probably acknowledges the priority of the Muse cult in the north and the derivative status of that of Helikon. It would seem here again that the only Helikonian Muses are those of Hesiod and that their cult and festival are inextricably bound up in the history of the Hesiodic corpus.

Immediately after the list of the Muses we are given accounts of two groups of men with whom they are specially linked—kings (*basileis*) and bards (*aoidoi*). There is an interesting contrast of usage between Homer and Hesiod with regard to words for kingship. In the *Iliad*, basileis are local kings, exclusive and hereditary (or pseudohereditary) monarchs, who are for purposes of the Trojan expedition provisionally subordinate to Agamemnon, himself commonly given the title *wanaks* (an archaic and poetic word for "ruler"). This last term is also used of various other Iliadic and Odyssean heroes as well as gods. The Homeric basileis, however, are always human, never divine. In Hesiod, on the other hand, basileis may be men *or* gods. Confined to the human plane in Homer, the designation is extended in Hesiod to the projections and legitimations of those human rulers on the level of the divine. Thus at the heart of the Hesiodic corpus the term *basileus* usurps much of the territory of Homeric *wan-*

aks (though this term is used by Hesiod as well, often in formulas shared with Homer), and the Homeric term for exclusively *human* authority becomes generalized to designate all authority. The theogonic tradition is in this sense the more humanist of the two and here as elsewhere views the divine from an insistently human perspective.

Hesiod's basileis are the managerial class, the rich and powerful on both the primary (human) and secondary (divine) planes. They are the "lords of the castle" who take so many forms in preindustrial society, the concentrators of wealth and wielders of authority. As we shall see, the overriding and fundamental distinction between the Hesiodic and Homeric perspectives is one of class. Homer views the world from the perspective of the managerial class, constantly affirming, both explicitly and implicitly, the legitimacy of authority. Hesiod's most characteristic perspective is refreshingly antithetical to Homer's and is that of the victims rather than the wielders of power.

But one of the strategies for survival of the victims of power—not the most attractive—is adulation, and that is the one dramatized in the prooimion (though the more characteristically cynical Hesiodic voice is heard even here). The Muse Kalliope—identified in the tradition with epic poetry, though Hesiod does not make explicit the individual responsibilities of the Muses—is said to "serve both kings and bards" (80). The most obvious link would seem to be that bards *use* poetry to sing the praise of kings—that is, after all, the principal function of much of archaic Greek poetry (see Nagy 1979, 222ff.)—but that is not the one developed here. Rather, Hesiod puts both kings and bards under the direct protection of Kalliope as if both were singers, or, rather, as if the rhetorical skills of the kings were the important ones, and their authority a function of their verbal abilities. The "sweet

dew" the Muses place in the mouth of the infant basileus is
the gift that grants authority. And then, just look at the shift
of perspective:

> And the people,
> all of them, look to him as he hands down judgments
> with uncrooked justice. And he speaks without fault,
> quickly and wisely putting an end even to a big
>   dispute.
> That's why there are kings called "reasonable"—
>   because
> they easily reverse the fortunes of people wronged in
>   public disputes,
> exerting their persuasion with gentle words.
>
>   [84–90]

The lines immediately following those quoted here have been
cited above (p. 21) to illustrate the interpenetration of Homeric and Hesiodic language. Even in his most adulatory
mode, this speaker views the ruler from the perspective of
the ruled. The king as rhetor is the essential manifestation of
kingship because it is through speaking that the king can right
wrongs, resolve disputes, and come to the aid of the op-
pressed. In fact, his power to do good is a function of his
abilities as a speaker, and that is the gift of the Muses. The
parallel praise of bards (94–103), though not rigorously sym-
metrical with that of kings, associates the two as correctors
of ills, but now Zeus is invoked as the divinity with special
bonds to kings, while the bards are associated with Apollo
and the Muses. As the honeyed voice of the king brings solace
to the victim of injustice, that of the bard, singing of gods
and heroes, brings relief from anguish and worries. This is a
rather unexpected parallelism, and not at all the kind of praise
of kings and self-advertisement of bards familiar from the *Iliad*

and *Odyssey.* Again Hesiod's emphasis is on the failure of the world of our immediate experience and of the various specifically human skills that offer some correction to that failure. Both king and bard emerge as therapists functioning in the context of the general misery of the human condition. The king fulfills his (divine) function to the extent that he serves our need to be protected from one another; the bard fulfills his by using the evasive ingenuities of art to remove us from the immediate experience of a reality the brute facts of which are inseparable from "anguish and worries" (102).

The third and final summary of the contents of the *Theogony* closes the prooimion in the form of an invocation. Now we are indeed very close to the organization of the material as it will actually be spun out, starting with the children of Earth and Sky and Night and Sea. The stars and rivers are added to the list in a sentence (108–10) whose authenticity has been doubted. But what a loss if we were to omit it!

> And tell how in the first place the gods and the earth
>   came to be,
> and the rivers and the boundless sea with its seething
>   swell
> and the shining stars and wide heaven above,
> as well as the gods born of these, givers of good
>   things. . . .

This "earth" is Gaia and this "heaven" Ouranos. The rivers and the sea (Pontos) are likewise simultaneously deities and parts of the natural world. Much of the fascination of the *Theogony*—the very basis of its specifically poetic power—lies in this creative misuse of words, this doubling of the meanings of ordinary nouns like *earth* and *sky* to designate *not* what we all know they designate but rather primordial monster-gods, the rough antecedents of a human universe. Theogony and cosmogony are not to be separated here. The glue that binds them together is composed of language and imagination.

The Succession Myth and the Titanomachy

First of all, then, Khaos came to be. . . .

[116]

The poem opens with the answer to the question posed in the final verse of the prooimion, and the opening words are doubtless an echo, however distant, of the unrecoverable prototype that also lies behind the b'rešith ("In the beginning . . .") of Genesis. They constitute the rhetorical equivalent of that explosive and sublime phrase, and this momentary similarity serves to underline the radical differences between the two cosmogonies. Genesis is of course the monotheistic redaction of much disparate material, largely premonotheist, while in Hesiod the supremacy of a single priesthood (or a single god) has not intervened to mask and edit out the conflicts represented by the traditional creation stories and their attendant succession myths. If Genesis claims that "in the beginning" there was *one* entity, which then generated all the others by a succession of acts of will, the *Theogony* claims that the beginning of things—or perhaps it is better to say the first thing we can talk about—was a "gaping" (*khaos*), a division or separation. As a result of this rending or mutilation of some previous, and apparently ineffable or simply irrelevant, unity, the differentiation of reality as we know it began.

After Khaos (about whom we hear little more) come Earth (Gaia), Tartaros, and Eros. Hesiod has not really started the genetic account of the world at this point; he is simply dealing out the cards, the givens he needs to generate reality. Of these first entities, Eros is initially the most interesting, no doubt in part because the heritage of Freud has restored his status in a way that makes him the most credible, the most comprehensible of these primal deities. In fact, the (re-)mythification of Eros and Thanatos in the tradition of Freud provides a possible paradigm for what the Hesiodic tradition is doing before our eyes. Psychoanalysis gives these principles of human experience an (illusory) objective existence. They constitute enormously important *conditions* of that experience and as such transcend the life of the individual and emerge as generalized patterns that shape and determine human reality, which is to say, the world. In other words, what Hesiod did in the guise of art—the invention or definition of those entities that constitute the conditions of our being—Freud did as analytic psychology. That the two formulations share the entity Eros in a very fundamental role is not coincidental. The point I want to make here is that, with Freud's help, we can understand the sort of statement Hesiod makes in assigning a primal role to an entity called Eros. If we try to generalize from this and add Earth, Sea, Heaven, and so forth to this pantheon, we seem at first to be mixing incompatibles, but the clear meaning of this poem is that these entities are in some sense comparable, that they belong to the same realm of fundamentals. If from our perspective we can still imagine what Hesiod's gods might be, it is surely Eros that we can conceive in that role, and the best way to enter imaginatively into Hesiod's theology may well be to take Eros as our paradigm and try to imagine the other entities as divinities in the sense that we can apply that title to Eros.

Given this understanding of the *Theogony*, we must nevertheless be careful to avoid approaching the poem as a sort of outline sketch of the "collective unconscious" in its Hellenic manifestation. This view simply does not correspond to the realities of the poem. The poem is, first and foremost, an assertion of the power of poetry to contain, shape, and define the conditions of our being. The role of tradition in forming this particular poetic statement is vast, complex, and finally indefinable, but one thing is certain—that the tradition in question consists of *language,* and language is something learned. That is, the tradition we are looking at is man-made, and its evolution is not Darwinian but Lamarckian, as is all cultural evolution. The tradition is provisionally borne, changed, and then passed on by individuals each of whom enters the world a tabula rasa, at least as far as the traditional information is concerned. Acquired characteristics are transmitted to the next bearer in an unbroken creative chain. Thus the formulation is constantly renewed and belongs constantly to the present. We ourselves stand outside this tradition and see that all its formulations are subject to change and therefore provisional, yet they claim to be absolute—hence the inevitable internal contradictions. This is what I take to be the nature and tone of our *Theogony.* The power it claims is poetic power, bound up with but not limited by the claim of veracity. It is a creator and destroyer of myths and of mythical beings and conceives these entities as its possessions, to do with as it likes.

Whatever else Eros may be here, he is introduced ex nihilo at this early point as a structural principle absolutely essential to the genealogical model. He is the force of combination that unites the generative pairs, and there can be no theogony, properly speaking, until he is present.

We have already noted the peculiar fascination attached to the earliest figures sketched in the *Theogony.* They do indeed seem to be anthropomorphic entities taking shape out of raw matter before our eyes, as if Herodotos's naive account of

Homer's and Hesiod's personal creation of shapes for the gods were accurate and these passages represented the process in action.

Hesiod's Gaia (Earth) must be simultaneously a familiar physical presence—the earth itself—and an anthropomorphic (and more specifically gynecomorphous, or "woman-shaped") divinity. These simultaneous meanings create a unique tension within a single linguistic sign, a tension that is relieved to some extent in modern editions of the Greek, as well as in translations, by the use of capitalization. But to write *Earth* in one place and *earth* in another is only to make explicit a crude and misleading distinction. In fact a complex range of meanings extends from the fully gynecomorphous Gaia of the opening episodes of the *Theogony* to the other pole at which the word *gaia* designates the physical earth or some portion of it.

The characteristically Hesiodic epithet *pelore* is the key to the characterization of Gaia. It occurs describing *gaia* in roughly one fifth of the instances where a personified Earth is clearly implied. The word on which it is built, *pelor*, and its derivates occur commonly in Homer and in Hesiod, straddling several semantic fields largely distinct in English: that which is *pelorios* may be simply "huge" or it may be properly "monstrous" or again "prodigious." In Homer, these words may refer to that which is large or awe-inspiring but not specifically monstrous. In Hesiod, however, the *pelor* group is never used for things that are simply large. Aside from Gaia, adjectival forms describe the snake portion of Ekhidna and the sickle used to castrate Ouranos. The nouns refer exclusively to monsters, specifically Typhoeus (twice), Ekhidna, and the Gorgon. *Gaia pelore* then is not simply big, not simply huge—she is monstrous, and the repeated, strident, pejorative epithet is as strongly determinative of our response to Gaia as the similarly insistent "(big) fool" (*[mega] nepie*) is of our response to Hesiod's brother. Moreover, it has long been noticed that the pelor group of epithets bind together Mother Earth and her huge, unruly offspring, the Giants. In her aspect as *Gaia pelore*, "monstrous Earth," she is specifically linked to the destructive forces represented by the Giants and Typhoeus. If I have taken so much time over this Greek word, it is because the available English translations regularly misrepresent it, dulling its pejorative force. But Hesiod's Mother Earth is a much more vicious creature than these translations imply, and her viciousness is summed up in the repeated epithet.

When she is first evoked, Earth is described not as "monstrous" but as "broad-breasted," a word that occurs only here. This is, though, a special situation, and Gaia is found here in a list of toponyms—Khaos, Earth, and Tartaros. This is the first stage in the process of her anthropomorphization. She is not yet explicitly a human-shaped entity, and the odd epithet itself introduces the first hint that she is becoming one. The decidedly nonanthropomorphic descriptive phrase that follows immediately ("solid foundation of all things forever," 117) reinforces the paradox and draws attention to the violent split that has come about in the significance of the word *gaia*.

What follows is a catalog of offspring; the genealogical model in fact creates the gynecomorphous Gaia, and not the other way round. Finally, with the birth of Kronos, one of this string of entities begins to take on human spiritual as well as physical characteristics:

> After these the last one born was crooked-thinking
>   Kronos,
> most terrible of the children, and he detested his virile
>   begetter.
>
> [137–38, cf. 155]

Something fundamentally and unambiguously human has entered at last—hate—and the chilling fact is that it is hate, Oedipal hate, that is the first truly human trait that we see this poem project into the realm of the divine. This hate further infects all the rest of the siblings and procreators in the genealogical myth, and they become human (or perhaps we should say humanoid) as a result of it. It is specifically as the object of Ouranos's sadistic brutality—"he delighted in his foul deed" (158)—that Gaia is first characterized as "monstrous." As he thrusts their offspring back inside her and the monster-woman groans at the horrible pain ("monstrous Earth groaned within, stretched" 159–60), her immediate response is an evil one:

> . . . she invented a treacherous and evil trick.
>
> [160]

And most striking of all is that her own joy at the prospect of her imminent revenge takes on a sadistic aspect exactly balancing Ouranos's attitude, and *that* is precisely when she is again called "monstrous." Kronos promises to act:

> So he spoke. Monstrous Earth rejoiced greatly in her heart.
>
> [173]

As we have seen, Gaia is described as "monstrous" repeatedly, but the tone is set here, and it is this vicious victim that will be evoked as "monstrous Earth" later (though she may then be in the service of potential justice). The epithet comes up three times in the Typhoeus episode (820–80), where, as she produces one last antagonist to challenge Zeus, she is at her most terrible. At that point the epithet even spills over to be applied to *gaia* where the word apparently designates simply the physical earth.

Thus the narratives in which Gaia is unambiguously gynecomorphous place her in roles that are grotesque and vicious—the appropriate match for her child and consort, Ouranos. Though she is the victim of Ouranos's enormous jealousy of the potential power of his offspring and though the brutality of her victimization is extreme, she does not have the sympathy of the Hesiodic voice. She responds to a "foul deed" with an "evil trick" (158–60).

We may look ahead a bit at this point and place this rather surprisingly threatening Mother Earth in context. The progression in the *Theogony* from a universe ruled by crude and violent forces of nature to one in which the ruling forces are anthropomorphic and essentially human has often been appreciated (see Kirk 1962b, 93ff.). In the "fable" (*ainos*) of the *Works and Days* (202–12 with 274–81), the further crucial distinction is made between the world of nature, where justice (*dike*) is absent, and that of culture, characterized by the presence of justice as a realizable force. In the *Theogony*, Ouranos and Gaia represent the antithesis of the ideal of human society ruled by dike. They represent a vision of the fundamental state of the universe as an unstable tension between male lust and jealously hoarded power on the one hand, and on the other, ultimately triumphant female rage and resentment at subjection to that lust and power—a rage that finally destroys the sexuality and by the same stroke the anthropomorphic identity of the male partner. At this stage, though, true dike simply does not exist. This is a world of comic-book horror, beyond good and evil, or, rather, before the introduction of justice and hence irremediably monstrous.

The grotesque enormity of this vicious victim, whose revenge for her own victimization is cosmic in scale, is in a sense a projection of the extreme misogyny that characterizes the *Works and Days* and that will occupy us later. Here, however, in the *Theogony*, there is no indication that the male standpoint is championed and the female judged inferior. The only positive moral force, the only possibility for the creation of a tolerable universe ruled by justice, lies in the future, in the offspring of the primal couple. Ouranos and Gaia are simply the equally monstrous forebears of an only potentially human universe.

Monstrous Earth is the archetypal mother of the *Theogony*, far surpassing all others in fertility and productivity. She is given credit for producing some thirty offspring, but many of them are such vague collective entities as "Mountains," "Furies," and "Giants" so that in fact her progeny is numberless. As the primal divine mother, she sums up the paradox of the genealogical model as it is applied to the gods. The gods are immortal, deathless (*athanatoi*). Before the first account of a birth in the *Theogony* the conventional epithet has been applied to them eight times, and it is clear that their deathlessness (understood to include freedom from the debilities of aging), here as in Homer, is the essence of their divinity. It is the single quality that excludes them definitively from the sphere of the human. But if they are deathless, they are not birthless, whatever the implied contradiction to the traditional and formulaic description of them as "existing forever" (for example, *aien eonton*, 21). They come to be in a reasonably orderly succession, and, for all practical purposes, with birth comes death, for them as for us, since a succession of births produces a succession of generations, each displacing its predecessor, so that each patriarch, at least, must fade to insignificance as his sons grow to occupy his place.

What is the genealogical model doing here, then, if it fits badly with the fundamental givens of traditional theology, themselves inextricably embedded in the traditional language of the poetry? An obvious answer is that the model is in fact a human one projected onto the screen of eternity. The most extreme form of this interpretation is associated with one of the earliest known writers of prose fiction, Euhemeros, who died about twenty-five years after Alexander the Great. In Euhemeros's novel (known today only from ancient summaries), a traveler discovered evidence on an island in the Indian Ocean proving that Ouranos, Kronos, and Zeus had in fact been kings who succeeded one another in a great dynasty that ruled in the distant past. As an account of where gods come from, Euhemerism has an obvious appeal, but one must be careful in applying it to the Greek theogony. In Hesiod, the generational scheme is clearly a fully developed poetic metaphor. Doubtless at some moment in the obscure Mesopotamian past the succession myth was indeed a projection in cosmic scale of human generations and dynastic succession, but this Hellenized form is something different. It is harnessed to the service of art rather than politics. If the coming-to-be of the world and the gods in Hesiod is modeled on the coming-to-be of the human family, it is primarily because the conditions of our existence are always, in Greek tradition, conceived in human terms. Hesiod's cosmos is human—or at least protohuman—before it is a cosmos, and the *Theogony* is the story of its progressive humanization.

Between the production of the four primal entities and the point where the generational metaphor takes hold are two series of parthenogenetic births. Khaos produces Erebos and Night, and this brother-sister couple in turn produces Aither and Day. But the poet has anticipated here—the children of Earth have priority over those of Khaos and Night—and the latter are set aside for nearly a hundred lines. Along with Mountains and Sea, Earth produces her consort Sky (*Ouranos*) and prepares the way for the generation of the Titans and the Olympians.

The passage on the offspring of Earth (126–210), where the Near Eastern succession myth takes shape in its distinctively humanized and dramatic Greek form, is one of the richest and most satisfying parts of the *Theogony*. We have seen that the characters are vivid in their monstrosity, and the moral world of their conflict is exceptionally clear. Gaia gives birth to eleven Titans before bringing forth Kronos, whose hate for his father equals—and finally surpasses—the father's hatred for his offspring. He volunteers to be the agent of his mother's evil plot and in a passage of extreme graphic brutality reaches out from his "ambush" and slashes off his father's genitals with his mother's sacrificial sickle of "gray adamant" (perhaps, but not certainly, to be identified as iron). What follows is a sublime and grotesque parody of impregnation as the rain of blood and semen impregnates Earth with Furies, Giants, and Ash-Tree Nymphs (*Meliai*). These last seem out of place, and there is no simple and satisfactory explanation for their inclusion at this point. Is this a simple allegory, elegantly telling us that the trees of the earth were incidental products of the violent act and the rain of blood and semen? As so often in the *Theogony*, some crucial association or symbolism seems simply to have been lost for us and with it the coherence of the mythic formulation. Yet ash trees have specifically Hesiodic associations that reach Virgil, who portrays the Askraean bard in what looks like an Orphic pose, luring the ash trees down the mountains with his song (*Eclogue* 6.69–71).

It is striking that thus far the *Theogony* has not reached the point where we must ask about the relationship between poetic myth and institutionalized cult, since few of these first deities seem to have had important independent cults at an early date. With the account of the birth of Aphrodite (188–206), we enter into a new realm of theological poetry, one in which the poetry must seemingly have been limited in its inventiveness by the resistant canonizations of myth and symbolism that are characteristic of cult. The relationship is, however, largely unrecoverable. The poem is evasive, and one suspects here another mutual parasitism of cult and poetic tradition. In giving prominence to Kythera and Cyprus, the poem *seems* to be acknowledging two major cult sites of Aphrodite, but again the question whether the myth created the local cults or the cults the myth is unanswerable, and the principal thrust of the passage is the explanation of a series of epithets of the goddess. That is, the words themselves generate the stories. (This is the process that a nineteenth-century student of ancient lore was describing when he asserted that "myth is a disease of language.")

When the severed genitals, covered with blood and semen, land in the sea, they float, surrounded and perhaps supported by a "white foam" (*leukos aphros*), so that the girl who mysteriously emerges from them—one appreciates the prim symbolism of Botticelli's cockleshell—is "She-of-the-foam," (*Aphrodite*). The name is even glossed as "foam-born (*aphrogenea*), for the slow-witted in the audience, and the relationship of name and story is further elaborated. She sailed past Kythera off the southeast tip of the Peloponnese, and that is why she is called "Kythereia" (though the superficially credible explanation of a local cult title is called in question by a difference in vowel quantity between *Kythēra* and *kythĕreia*). Finally, she is "Kyprogenea" because she eventually came ashore on Cyprus. Now Cyprus and Kythera had early cults of Aphrodite, as later writers (inevitably influenced by Hesiod) assert and as the archaeological record seems to confirm. But there is sublexical play here as well. The first syllables of these place-names (Cy-, Ky-) are identical in Greek, and that syllable (with the sound *KŪ*) has a wealth of erotic associations. The verb *kuo* means, among other things, "to impregnate," and its stem generates a number of obscenities and obscene puns in Attic comedy. The special relationship between these place-names and Aphrodite is thus embedded in the syllables of their names. As the account of the various names of the goddess continues, we learn that she is also called "She-who-loves-the-(male)-genitals"—or simply "she-who-is-intimately-associated-with-the-genitals" (*philommedes*), and the explanation of this epithet is that "she emerged out of the genitals" (200). What is clearly the same epithet appears a half-dozen times in Homer as *philommeides*— the difference has been inaudible to most Greek speakers of most periods—conveniently understood as "She-who-loves-laughter." That this is a rather precious, pretty bowdlerization is clear, but its date and the history of the interaction of the two epithets is not. This entire account is one of the striking points of conflict between Homeric and Hesiodic theogonic lore: Homer's Aphrodite is a daughter of Zeus and Dione— and Olympian—while Hesiod's is a Titan of a sort.

The richly worked passage on Aphrodite is a good example of the way the Hesiodic voice insists on the centrality of language and finally of poetry in its account of the world. There are dozens of explanations of words—what are usually called "etymologies"—here, some of them explicitly spelled out and others woven into the fabric of the narrative. Their accuracy or inaccuracy by standards of modern historical linguistics is utterly irrelevant. In the context of archaic Greek poetry, these associations of words are real and meaningful. It is not so much that words are keys to the things they designate (as the etymological tradition from Plato's *Cratylus* to Isidore of Seville asserted) as that words and their components generate stories, patterns of association that are the stuff of poetry. Conceived in this way, poetic theology maintains its virtual immunity from institutionalization. Even the names of the gods dissolve into patterns of sound whose manipulation is the domain of poets and whose secrets are articulated only through them.

Once the Titans are introduced and primal Eros redefined as the servant of Aphrodite, the narrative reverts to the level of the first beings and gives an account of the offspring of Night (211–32). This striking passage constitutes an archaic account of the origins of negativity, of evil, an account whose importance for the early history of Greek thought has been recognized. If the generation of Ouranos and Gaia was essentially divorced from the human and so beyond the realm of good and evil, this largely allegorical scheme of associations goes directly to human concerns, exploiting the genealogical model in its principal function: to answer the question, "Where does X come from?" In a sense, of course, the entire *Theogony* is an elegant poetic catalog of traditional answers to that protophilosophical question. Centuries later, the Hellenistic poet Kallimakhos was to write an influential poem entitled simply "Causes" (*Aitia*), which was a transposition of this same sort of poetry to a new philosophical and aesthetic context.

Night's first offspring are, not surprisingly, Death, Sleep, and Dreams, intimately associated with the Fates and with various manifestations of doom. The sexual politics of Hesiod are obtrusive here. It is a female, Night, that stands at the source of the evils of the universe (conceived as the bitterly felt limitations set to our own existence), and it is one of her female offspring, Eris (Strife) that—still parthenogenetically—produces the string of specifically human ills, including Labor, Famine, Suffering, Battles, Murder, Carnage, and Lawlessness. We have here as well an implied contrast between the two sorts of manifestation of death in Greek myth distin-

guished by Jean-Pierre Vernant: the female, destructive entities, such as Battle, Carnage, and the Furies, that rend and
tear, as against Death (*thanatos*) *him*self, whose brothers are
Sleep and Dreams and whose gentleness is depicted so ex-
quisitely on the famous Euphronios krater of the Metropolitan
Museum of Art.

Following the list of these all-too-human children of
Night, the poem makes another radical transition, turning
this time to populate the world with monsters, all sprung
from Pontos (Sea), one of the parthenogenetic children of
Gaia, and from his descendants. This list is exceptionally long
(233–336), containing more than seventy-five new entities,
one every 1¼ lines. Clearly there is not much space here for
development of individual characterization and stories, and
the list that succeeds this one, that of the rivers and streams
sprung from the Titans Tethys and Okeanos, is denser still:
twenty-five rivers and forty-one streams are named in thirty-
three lines, a representative sample, the narrative voice tells
us, of the total of three thousand springs and three thousand
rivers—but to get all the names straight, you would have to
ask the locals (370).

It is exceptionally difficult to communicate the qualities
of this poetry of lists and catalogs, but at the same time it is
important to remember that this sort of performance is clearly
something that the Hesiodic voice revels in. To fit this flood
of proper names to the demands not just of the meter but of
the poetry is a task that leaves us in awe of the workings of
this tradition. Did this list come forth slightly differently in
every performance, or was a passage of this density essentially fixed for all time? There is no way to give a definitive
answer, but the tendency of the lists to contradict one another—the Moirai are parthenogenetic children of Night at
line 217 and daughters of Zeus and Themis at lines 904–6—

suggests a certain rigidity in the set pieces that has not been
wholly reduced to consistency in the composite that is our
Theogony. If we look at it from an aesthetic point of view, we
can guess that the pleasure its intended audience took in the
list poetry must have had affinities both with the pleasure we
find in the patter songs of Gilbert and Sullivan and with the
Joycean delight in lists that pervades *Ulysses* and *Finnegans
Wake.* Hesiod's lists do not translate well (as I suspect Joyce's
do not, either), since their charm lies in rhythm and in the
play of tiny, sublexical units of meaning, along with the evoc-
ative power of the names themselves. A few modern poets
have explored the rhetoric of the list, most notably John Ash-
bery ("Into the Dusk-Charged Air," in *Rivers and Mountains*)
and Kenneth Koch, who has found the poetry of lists to be a
mode easily accessible to children. Their rewritings of Hesiod
are belated and ironic. They are perhaps closer to the Hellenistic poets who appreciated and appropriated Hesiod than to
the Hesiodic corpus itself—but one must always be wary of
the traditional tendency to look in Hesiod for a ground of
sincerity contrasting with the elegant ironies of his imitators.
He is no less an imitator than they, no less conscious of his
distance from the remote and elusive sources of truth, no
more willing to be subjected to reduction and appropriated
as a bearer of a truth separable from his words.

Hesiodic lists and catalogs range from the dense sequence of names of rivers and streams to the partially preserved *Catalogue of Women,* whose entries (typically opening
with the formula "Or such as she who . . .") seem to have
varied greatly in length. The *Shield of Herakles* is an expansion
of the Alkmene entry and runs to nearly five hundred lines,
but most of the entries would seem to have been shorter. This
idiosyncratic predilection of the Hesiodic corpus for lists has
led to the suggestion that there was a "Boeotian school" of

poetry that took special pride in its lists and catalogs. As with most generalizations of this sort, the evidence supporting this one is ambiguous and susceptible to other interpretations. Still, before we shrug off the Boeotian school too lightly, it is well to keep in mind the striking fact that Boeotia and adjacent Thessaly receive unexpectedly generous representation in the Iliadic catalog of ships (*Il.* 2.484–759) and the Odyssean catalog of women of the heroic period (*Od.* 11.235–330) (cf. Kirk 1962b, 69).

The lists that proliferate in the genealogical scheme of the *Theogony* place us repeatedly in the presence of bizarre and lovely juxtapositions of various sorts of traditional material, along with allegories and elaborated etymologies. The result is a poetic whole that defies and prohibits analysis, though at one extreme it seems to anticipate the elegant poetry of Alexandria in its delight in wordplay and proper names, while at another it seems to tap the folk traditions that were to produce the Norse Eddas:

> And Keto, last of all, after mating with Phorkys,
> gave birth to the terrible snake that guards the golden
>   apples,
> in the caverns of the dark earth at the great boundaries.
> [333–35]

Cosmogony and theogony continue to be bound together as the account of the offspring of the Titans goes on to include Sun, Moon, Dawn, Winds, and Morning Star. The spectacle of a world—imaginative, psychological, ethical, and physical—rushing to completion is breathtaking. It is the interruptions to this massive development, though, that hold our attention, perhaps most of all the remarkable elaboration on Hekate (411–52). This is the Hesiodic voice at its richest and most bizarre, ample reason of course for the passage to have been alternately condemned as an interpolation and exalted as an indication of Hesiod's *real* concerns. It is possible, however, to restore a unitarian reading here without recourse to a personal Hesiodic voice if we explain this rich elaboration in terms of the thematic organization and thrust of the *Theogony* as a whole. It then becomes clear that Hekate receives the prominence she does here as a representative of the old order projected into the new and as a cult figure pointing to the relationship between Hesiodic theology and human interests and concerns (Griffith 1983, 51–55). The *Theogony* to this point has remained aloof from cult, as we have seen, asserting the theological primacy of poetry. But this is only possible up to a point in speaking about divinities—the realities of cult and popular piety must be given their due. That is just what the poem does with this centrally located hymn celebrating Hekate. It is a celebration of the *usefulness* of this deity (whose unpretentious and popular cult is richly attested, particularly in Aristophanes), of her potential to serve her devotees.

The Hekate hymn is located at the end of the rich proliferation of the Titanic offspring, just before the introduction of the most important and memorable of the grandchildren of Earth and Sky, that is, the children of Kronos and Rhea, the Olympians of the older generation. There are, finally, only two elaborated stories in this succession myth, Kronos's victory over Ouranos (154–210) and Zeus's victory over Kronos (453–506), followed by his consolidation of power. With the Hekate hymn came the acknowledgment of the role of cult, and now we are plunged directly among the institutionalized deities of the world from which this poetry emerges. The poetry never admits that its freedom is circumscribed, but there is a change of tone, of orientation, and from the moment when Zeus the liberator defeats Kronos the tyrant, the poem is dealing with a new kind of power, one that requires justification rather than exposure for the raw and arbitrary force that it is. Kronos learns that he is destined to be overthrown by his own son "by the will of Zeus" (465). The introduction of the inappropriate (or at least prematurely placed) formula amounts to an indication that the power of Zeus is simply a fact of this poem's environment, immune to the demands and limitations of the sequential narrative.

Here again, Bronze Age Anatolian material, and specifically the epic of Kumarbi, is echoed and seems to be brought into less-than-perfect harmony with the tradition that asserted the Cretan origin of Zeus (see West 1966, 290–93). The motif of the swallowed stone (known and advertised by the poem as a Delphic institution) is shared with the Hittite material and seems to render superfluous Rhea's flight and concealment in the Cretan cave. Nevertheless, the accounts are juxtaposed, and we are simply and rather vaguely told that Kronos was defeated by craft and by force (496) and that the maliciously swallowed children were vomited up in reverse order, starting with the stone that had been substituted for Zeus. The consolidation of power is anticipated in a similarly elliptical account of Zeus's liberation of his bound uncles, presumably the Kyklopes, whose gift of the thunderbolt is said to be the foundation of that power.

It is at this point that the poem introduces mankind, and the logic of the progression seems clear. Pre-Olympian poetic theology, mediated by the Hekate hymn, has ceded to the institutionalized myth that is bound to the conditions of life in the present-day world. This is where man belongs and this is where he is introduced, but for our purposes it will be useful to set this passage aside for the moment, long enough to look briefly at the long recapitulation of the consolidation of Zeus's power (617–885) and the further elaborations of the

genealogical scheme (886–1022). However crucial and central
to the *Theogony* the rebellious Titans' aid to mankind and the
consequences of that aid may be, the passage constitutes a
sort of window within the larger genealogical narrative, looking out on a brutal but familiar world decidedly different from
the stage of the larger narrative. When Prometheus and Pandora disappear from the scene (616), we are plunged back
into the world of sublime and monstrous violence far beyond
human scale that is the invisible substrate of the sheltered
realm of our experience.

There is, however, a significant change of scene at this
point, and when the confrontation between Zeus and the Titans begins, the theater of action is explicitly the great Thessalian plain, with Zeus entrenched in his stronghold on
Mount Olympos to the north and the Titans fighting from
Mount Othrys to the south. In other words, the geography
of this world-in-formation has become highly specific, and the
crucial confrontation is located in the heartland of Greek
myth, the landscape that was the home of Jason and of Akhilleus. The confrontation itself is left extremely vague, both
in its motivation and in its development. The sequence of
events is unclear, but at some point in the ten years of fighting, at Gaia's urging Zeus releases the Hundred-handers, Bri-
areus and his brothers, from their prison (cf. 147–53) and at
the end of the ten years, with their crucially important aid,
defeats the Titans.

In a corpus characterized by extremes, the poetry of this
battle narrative stands out as extraordinary. If the grim and
visceral battle poetry of the *Iliad* is echoed in modern novels
of war, the stylistic heirs of Hesiod's war narrative belong to
the genre of Frank Herbert's *Dune*. The scale of the description is overwhelming and finally numbing. The archaic song
of star wars and cosmic battle is amazingly modern in its

giddy, outrageous scale and the enormity of the events described.

> The boundless sea groaned terribly,
> the earth crashed and wide heaven resounded,
> shaken, while great Olympos was rocked to its roots
> by the onslaught of the immortals—a heavy pounding
>   of feet
> reached misty Tartaros with the sharp crash
> of the limitless rout and the powerful missiles.
>
> [678–83]

The entire passage is a struggle of revelation, of manifestation of violence and power (649–50, 689), and the poetry itself assaults all the senses, but principally the eye and the ear.

When it is all over, the poem takes us to the place of confinement of the defeated Titans, the underworld, the description of which is elaborated on a huge scale (717–819) in catalog form. Many of the entities now located here have been met before among the children of Night, but now these horrors have a *place*—they are specifically and explicitly distanced from our world, which becomes by implication more tolerable for their absence. But if this is a threatening landscape populated by monsters, its description contributes as well to the increasing orderliness of this nascent cosmos and to its moral coherence. The longest element in the description is that concerned with the Styx (775–807), the most striking feature of this underworld and its ethical center as the principal guarantee of the good faith of the immortals. The prominence of this creature—both river and goddess—is a function of the cynicism and realism of the Hesiodic conception of power. That these fundamentally lawless superhuman entities should take into consideration any factor beyond their own immediate gratification in the exercise of their vast powers is something that requires explanation. It is the Styx, privileged to serve as their oath, that keeps them honest.

After the stylistic tour de force of the Titanomachy, the poem rises to one last climax of outrageous violence, cosmic in scale. In the Typhoeus episode (820–80), Gaia, now again repeatedly described as "monstrous," gives birth to her ultimate creation, a thing with ray-gun eyes and a hundred snake heads capable of generating a huge repertory of hideous noises. When he hisses, the mountains echo.

> And HE would have ruled over mortals and immortals,
> if the father of gods and men had not quickly noticed.
>
> [837–38]

In the struggle, the sea boils, the earth melts—the smelting simile (861–66) is one of the most suggestive in the corpus— and Typhoeus is finally cast into Tartaros with the Titans, whence his violence manifests itself in our world in the form of the violent and unruly winds (as distinct from orderly Notos and his brothers).

After this last threat is dealt with by Zeus in one-to-one combat, the poem makes another odd shift (881–85). Now Gaia—whose counsel is always good, even if her actions are repellent—is suddenly placed back on the side of Zeus. Following her advice, the Olympians invite Zeus to rule over them, and when he parcels out their various rights and privileges (885) we may take it that the current order has been established and legitimated.

Clearly, though, something more is needed. Of the twelve canonical Olympians, Athena, Apollo, Artemis, Ares, Hermes, Hephaistos, and Dionysos still do not exist, and of course when the possibilities of elaboration along allegorical lines are added to the vast body of traditional material feeding into this poem, the potential for expanding it becomes literally infinite.

The poem as we have it, though, works through a catalog of Zeus's offspring and those of his siblings to an essentially independent catalog of the loves and children of goddesses who mated with mortals. Some of the entities introduced here seem to echo the concerns of a time rather more recent than we are accustomed to place "Hesiod," but that need not concern us. As it makes its transition to the *Catalogue of Women*— perhaps the oldest and most traditional of all this material— this poem has long since established its indifference to our attempts to pin it down to a historical moment and an authentic individual voice. It has asserted its power over the entire tradition of theology—power to invent and power to confirm—power, finally, to tell the truth if and when it pleases.

Gods and Men

At a specifiable moment in the history of the Greek worldview the gods became good. This seems on the surface an odd state of affairs. Given that the Bronze Age and the archaic period had left to the Greeks of the age of Perikles certain traditions about eternal beings possessing great power to affect our lives, and given that these traditions had been the stuff of poetry and art (while at the same time they played a central role in that more blatant theater of power, the cults and their temples and priests)—given all this, *why* should the demand suddenly be made that these gods be *good* and not simply powerful and capricious, as the archaic tradition portrayed them? This is nevertheless the essence of Sokrates' critique of archaic theology (= poetry) in Plato's *Republic*.

The poems of Homer and Hesiod portray the gods as

changeable, irresponsible, and frequently hostile to individuals or groups of men. Plato's Sokrates called for a new mythology free of these "defects," and the principle of the essential goodness and benevolence of the divine became a central dogma of all subsequent Greek theology (permeated as that tradition of theology is by Platonism). Presented in this way, the shift appears arbitrary, unmotivated, but of course Sokrates' demands are to be understood in the larger context of Platonic ontology and metaphysics. What primarily concerns us here is the aesthetic dimension of this revolution. The gods of the Greeks, as we have seen, belonged first of all to the poets, and any theological innovation would be experienced primarily as an aesthetic, poetic innovation—indeed, the Sokrates of the *Republic* attacks the problem in precisely these terms.

It is difficult, from a modern perspective, to conceive of this intimate association of the spheres of art and religion, and our difficulty arises primarily from the extraordinary power of the institution of the Christian church during the past millennium and a half of European cultural history. The major poets who have entered the arena of symbols that is the property of the church are, though conspicuous, relatively few in number. Dante and Milton became, in retrospect, emblematic of the Christianity of their respective cultures. Blake, surely the most powerful of the European theological poets since Hesiod, is the only one to generate a wholly new mythology while asserting his Christianity, and though the church has successfully assimilated him into the hymnal, it is clear that Blake resists this institutionalization and remains remotely idiosyncratic, to the point that to debate his heresy or orthodoxy would be superfluous. The poets are powerless to change the institution and, from Blake's time onward, increasingly isolated. For the past century art has repeatedly claimed to be the heir, the replacement for religion (in manifestations as various as those of Richard Wagner and Wallace Stevens). Institutionalized Christianity and the activity of art seem irreconcilably alienated, the received symbols of religion unavailable for further imaginative elaboration.

We cannot think this history away, but we must try. Perhaps we can best do so by putting religion from our minds entirely and looking to an art form with only the remotest (though that may also be to say the most insidious) pretense to significance beyond the level of entertainment. I am thinking of the science-fiction film, and, bathetic though the analogy may be, this is an art form that in recent years has developed in directions that distantly recall the conflicting forces in Greek theological poetry. The myths of the Greeks were, after all, essentially creative fantasies about the more-than-human in its relation to the human, and the same could be said of *The War of the Worlds* and of *ET*. The former, along with *The Thing, The Body Snatchers, Alien,* and other "archaic" and archaizing manifestations of the genre, projects extraterrestrials as sublime, subversive, destructive, and resolutely alien. In *ET* and its kin, the same aliens have become homey, benevolent, loving, and lovable. Put somewhat differently, the Gnostic fantasies of an Orson Welles—located in a universe where the only god-in-residence is Leviathan—compete with visions of a sustaining universe whose relationship to the absolute is mediated by the benevolent ET. In the fifth century, Sokrates' revisionist reading of earlier theology had a similar thrust in its rejection of the archaic worldview.

The point of the comparison is this: a culture in search of portraits of the gods compatible with the Platonic principle of the providential benevolence of the divine will find the Hesiodic account profoundly unsatisfactory—or, to put it in aesthetic terms, will find it ugly. Essential to the archaic Greek worldview is the down-to-earth perception that power is (among other things) irresponsibility—absence of accountability—and therefore that absolute power is absolute irresponsibility. This perception pervades the Homeric poems and even more conspicuously the Hesiodic, and it is fundamentally irreconcilable with post-Platonic theology, which from this perspective can only be seen as an apology for power. Hesiod's fantasies of the divine *other* are not warm or attractive fantasies. They are utterly innocent of the theological demand that the gods favor mankind or work in man's interests, and they are founded on a vision of the relationship of the very powerful to the very weak—that is, of the infinite, arbitrary, and indifferent force of the limits of desire to the feeble, ephemeral impulses of desire itself.

The divine remains inexorably *other*, and this is the essence of Hesiod's humanism. The Zeus of tradition is far from philanthropic, as the myths conveyed by both Homer and Hesiod make abundantly clear. Hesiod's universe comprises three primary elements: man, god, and the world. The natural environment—the physical conditions that constitute the immediate limitation (and potential source) of human sustenance and happiness—is hostile. In nature's perverse failure to sustain man the gods are deeply implicated:

> The gods have hidden man's livelihood and keep it hidden.
>
> [*W&D* 42]

These gods are portrayed consistently in the *Theogony* and only slightly less so in the *Works and Days* as the jealous enemies of mankind, eternal, capricious powers that elect an adversary relationship with their subjects, their victims, the creatures-of-a-day, and so emerge as self-indulgent cosmic bullies (when they are not expending their energies in the sublime mode of internecine conflict on a cosmic scale, totally beyond our interests and so beyond good and evil).

Then there is the third factor in the equation, mankind, and it is hard to imagine a reader of Hesiod who will fail to see that in both the major surviving poems (though the one is explicitly a tale of the gods and the other an account of man in the context of the natural world and the society he forges against that world), it is man, man's interests, man's culture, man's responsibility that are in fact central. In a sense each poem explores our relation to the nonhuman—the divine on the one hand, the world on the other—and in each instance finds the nonhuman wanting, inadequate, subhuman. The resolution of both these dilemmas is found in the full realization of human responsibility, alone capable of redeeming (and so rendering tolerable) the nonhuman (cf. Solmsen 1949, 86). Looking ahead for a moment to the *Works and Days*, we see that the farmer—man experiencing the brutal facts of his relationship to the physical world—must *decide* to *work* and beyond that must have certain cultural information at his disposal to render that work effective. The individual in his relations with others and confronted with the whole range of possibilities of human action must *choose justice* and at the same time keep before the mind's eye the corrective—and intensely imaginatively involving—spectacle of the consequences of unleashed absolute and irresponsible power.

What it comes down to is finally that, viewed from the perspective of the consequences for man—and there *is* no other perspective—it is justice (*dike*) that is central to Hesiod's imaginative universe rather than Zeus. And dike is not a goddess but a mode of human action, the object of a human choice. The deliberate association of Zeus with dike in the *Works and Days* is perhaps the single point at which we are placed most problematically in the presence of the unique moral vision of the Hesiodic corpus. The spectacle is just the opposite of the redemption of mankind by Zeus through dike. Rather, it is the redemption of the Zeus of tradition, through dike, by poetry—poetry that insists incessantly on its humanity, on its sympathy for the victims of power.

Human interests penetrate the *Theogony* explicitly only in the rather short passage we have left aside for consideration here—the account of the fate of Iapetus and Klymene's four sons, the four second-generation Titans whose rebellion and punishment are sketched out to serve as a paradigm for the unspecified crimes of their uncles and cousins (507–616). The passage begins with the punishments. They, after all, are the point here, as the poem sets out to give an account of Zeus's consolidation of power. Of Atlas and Menoitios we learn only that the first was "dauntless" (509) and that Zeus set him at the end of the world near the Hesperides to hold up the sky— the fact that at lines 746ff. we will find him performing the same function but standing in Tartaros presents no real problem of consistency—while Menoitios was "criminal" (514) and "too proud" (510) and therefore was knocked into Erebos by a thunderbolt. The third brother, Epimetheus, is simply identified as a "dolt" (511) for accepting the "fabricated girl-woman" (513–14) from Zeus. His crime—or rather his mistake—is spelled out where we would expect to find his punishment, perhaps because the two are in fact identical, or at least inseparable. Prometheus's punishment, though, is spelled out in great detail—the cruel bondage, the mutilating eagle, even the eventual release by Herakles to the greater glory of Zeus's offspring. But if Epimetheus starts out with a crime and no explicit punishment, his brother starts out with a punishment but no spelled-out crime beyond the fact that he was "cunning" (521) and tested his wits against Zeus (534).

The sequence of revelation of the elements of this traditional story—the essential Hesiodic myth, in that for purposes of archaic Greek tradition it seems to have belonged exclusively to Hesiodic poetry—is thus governed by the sort of contrasts and juxtapositions this poetry clearly relishes. But since there are two versions of the Prometheus/Pandora story in Hesiod, one in each of the major poems, it will be useful simply to place them side by side in order to get a sense of that story's specifically Hesiodic form (as opposed to the more complex and perhaps more familiar Aeschylean one).

Theogony	Works and Days
Prometheus was crafty (511) and was punished by Zeus (521–25), but the eagle was eventually killed by Herakles and Prometheus was liberated (526–34).	
At Mekone, when a settlement was made between gods and men, Prometheus divided the sacrificial animal and piled the good meat under the unattractive skin, the useless bones under the rich and desirable fat, and invited Zeus to choose (535–49). Although Zeus was *not* deceived, he still chose the bones and resented being cheated (550–61).	
Therefore, he withheld fire	Zeus hid fire because Pro-

from mankind, but Prometheus stole some fire and delivered it to man (562–70).

metheus had cheated him (48–50). Prometheus stole it back, and Zeus, furious, promised man some evil in return, "an evil they will cherish" (57–59).

In revenge, Zeus and Hephaistos created a woman (unnamed in this version). Athena clothed her and Hephaistos made her beautiful jewelry (571–84). Both men and gods were amazed at her charm (585–89).

Zeus had Hephaistos make a woman. All the gods gave some gift to this creation— hence her name, Pandora (60–82). Epimetheus accepted her in spite of Prometheus's earlier warnings about Zeus's gifts (83–89).

From her was born the cursed race of women, who live by the labor of men, like the drones in the beehive (590–602). Zeus added another curse: those who do not marry have no offspring, while those who do get at best a mixture of good and evil (603–12).

Before, there was no evil, no labor, no disease, but she took the top off the jar and released all of these, trapping only hope inside. Now the world is full of evils (90–104).

So Zeus cannot be tricked, and Prometheus still suffers (614–16).

There is no way to avoid what Zeus plans (105).

The distinction between gods and men seems to be blurred here. If Epimetheus accepted the woman, how did she bring miseries to mankind and not just to the Titans' offspring themselves? Or is Epimetheus really a man masquerading as a god—or an allegorical figure representing hindsight as Prometheus represents foresight? Comparative material abundantly demonstrates that the theft of fire from the gods by a trickster-hero is a widespread motif. Such tricksters often resemble these demigods in having superhuman characteristics. The Hesiodic form of the story requires these intermediate beings, if only so that the punishment of Prometheus may be superhuman in scale and horror. Once again, though, we find a story that seems to be out of place in its Hesiodic context and appears to be adapted rather crudely to the succession myth. In the *Works and Days*, where the succession myth is utterly irrelevant, still the genealogy of the heroes is explicitly consistent with the *Theogony*'s version of the story. Here, though, there is no punishment beyond human capacity. The tale requires only two levels of beings: suffering mortals and blissful, cruel gods. The form of the story we find in the *Theogony* is likewise somewhat contradictory. Prometheus is liberated at line 534, but eighty lines later he is said still to be suffering in chains. These problems suggest that what we have here is a tale of the culture-hero type, explaining simultaneously man's possession of fire and the wretchedness of the human condition. The Hesiodic tradition exploited this story in two different contexts; the *Theogony* is the one that required more adaptation.

In fact, the *Theogony* seems to accommodate the Prometheus story best *without* the Pandora story, which in any case is rather arbitrarily joined to it. Though the matter is not as clear as is sometimes claimed, Hesiod's Prometheus does seem to get his punishment primarily for his deception of Zeus regarding the allocation of the sacrificial meal and not for stealing fire. The meal at Mekone (apparently to be identified with Sikyon, near Corinth) in any case is the crucial episode in the *Theogony* presentation of Prometheus and the one of obvious relevance to the concerns of the poem. It is an extension of the development we have seen in the Hekate hymn in that it gives an account of cult—that is, of the relationship between gods and men. In doing so, the story's most obvious function is to provide an explanation of the cult practice of giving the fat and bones of sacrificial animals to the gods and the flesh and skins to men. The striking thing here is that what the poem gives us is a *comic* version of the explanation of this phenomenon. West (1966, 305) provides a list of the references to this commonplace in Attic comedy, where the point is always that man is corrupt, a scheming, hungry gut stopping at nothing for gratification. This is the comic vision of Aristophanes, and it is also Hesiod's, more conspicuously so in the *Works and Days*, but in the *Theogony* as well. There are, after all, other ways to explain the conventions of Greek sacrifice. The Homeric theology represents the gods as reveling in the *smell* of the burning fat—the *knise*, or "fat-smoke" that comes off the barbecue—and explains that they in fact *ate* nothing but nektar and ambrosia. This again offers a nice contrast between the Homeric and Hesiodic postures with reference to power, with Hesiod consistently adopting the perspective of the victim, the little guy, one of whose options, here as in Attic comedy, is to laugh at the powerful. In the folkloric context, this is the general thrust of the trickster tales to which we compared the Prometheus story.

In the *Theogony*, then, Prometheus is most conspicuously a trickster who takes the side of mankind and ensures that (at the cost of the valuable fat) man will at least get the most satisfying part of the sacrificial meal. The tensions within the Zeus theology of the Hesiodic corpus are conspicuous in the seemingly contradictory claim that Zeus was and was not deceived, but this problem is one we have encountered already.

Zeus's power and omniscience are givens of this poetry—
formulaic conventions of its language and fundamental no-
tions of the society that was its historical context—and these
givens are immune to the demands of narrative, though they
do not stand in the way of narratives with which they are
inconsistent.

This story generates another. When mankind got the best
part of the sacrificial meal, Zeus kept fire from us. I take it
that we *had* fire previously—the sacrificial meal presupposes
it—but that Zeus simply withdrew it. The poem is obscure
here, but the point may be that Zeus made firesticks useless
(though this requires taking the term *ash trees* in line 563 as a
kenning, or fixed metaphorical formula, for firesticks). Fire,
in any case, became unavailable, but the same philanthropic
minor deity, Prometheus, again infuriated Zeus by stealing
some fire and delivering it to mankind.

Zeus's second revenge is, of course, the creation of
women. It seems to me a mistake to speak of three separate
explanatory stories (*aitia*) here; at the very least we should
distinguish carefully among them. Certainly the story discussed above is an answer to the implied question, "Why do
we sacrifice as we do?" But what follows is entirely in answer
to the implied question, "Why is our life as miserable as it
is?" In other words, this story does *not* set out to give an
answer to the question where women came from, and its concerns are thus different from those of the second creation
account in Genesis, which it surpasses in misogyny. The first
two questions are part of the fabric of the *Theogony*, but the
third is not. This poem does not *care* where women came from
and turns its attention to this "lovely evil" only to elaborate
on the viciousness of Zeus's hostility to mankind and the
consequent wretchedness of the human condition. This may
seem an oversubtle point—indeed the same story in the *Works*

and Days can more credibly be read as an account of the relationship of men and women in society—but it is important
to realize here the extent of this tradition's misogyny. Women
are excluded from the sphere of discourse of the *Theogony.*
They themselves have no voice, and they are spoken about
only to explain the misery of the (male) human condition.

How are we to read Hesiod's misogyny? No one denies
its existence, and although it is possible to point to certain
contradictions within the Hesiodic representation of women,
there is general agreement that Hesiodic misogyny runs deep
and is a fundamental element of the constellation of attitudes
that constitutes the Hesiodic persona. It is easy to say simply
that traditional Greek society was (and is) sexually segre-
gated, that the public discourse of that society was that of
free, adult males, and the thrust of that discourse was often
misogynistic. The strategy of such an account is both devious
and transparent. When we find ourselves face to face with
attitudes we cannot in good conscience embrace, we step
aside and affect an objectivity that permits us to reduce them
to the status of quaint cultural peculiarities. Of course, we
are deeply implicated in this discourse, and that is why we
find it so fascinating. This account of the world that plays at
belonging to a dusty little Boeotian town some 2500 years ago
already embodies in full-blown form attitudes in which the
whole subsequent tradition of European literature is implicated and which we have only in the past generation learned
to qualify as "sexist."

A mode of criticism suited to the exposure and analysis
of these attitudes is in the process of creation. True, we have
had for a generation the Panofskys' study, *Pandora's Box,* in
which the history in the visual arts of that Hesiodic myth is
explored so brilliantly in its evolution from one elusive allegorical expression to another—all relentlessly pointing to the

idea the authors equally relentlessly refuse to articulate: the
female genitals are the source of all evil. But now something
more seems within reach. In a moment of creative crisis in
critical theory, feminist criticism has become the most progressive front. A vocabulary and a mode of analysis adequate
to the discussion of the sexual dimension of discourse are
being developed, and it is here if anywhere that a criticism is
to be found that embodies the potential to make creative
changes in our cultural tradition.

The poems of Hesiod are clearly of crucial importance
from this point of view, though their study in the light of
recent developments in critical theory is only beginning. The
most important advances thus far belong to the anthropolog-
ically influenced tradition of classical scholarship that owes
much to the pioneering work of Louis Gernet. In this vein,
Nicole Loraux (1978) and Marilyn B. Arthur (1982; 1983), in
particular, have explored Hesiodic misogyny with fascinating
results. Especially rich in its implications is Arthur's conclusion (1983, 112–16) that the *Theogony* dramatizes the construc-
tion of a realm that excludes woman—and that realm is first
of all the world of discourse itself (the sphere of *logos* as that
of the agora), and more specifically the realm of this poetry,
central to which is a fantasy of a world without women. But
are we talking about Hesiod here or about William Burroughs? Though she does not make the comparison, Arthur
nevertheless makes it clear that we are inevitably talking
about both and that the explicit and systematic misogynistic
fantasies of Burroughs's recent fiction are implicit in the very
discourse of Hesiod and in the way this tradition of poetry
understands the generation of texts.

A parallel line of scholarship has pursued both Hesiod's
theology and his sexism to their roots in socioeconomic conditions in archaic Greece on the principle that "it is in human

society and human history that we might try to seek out the
reasons for the degradation of Pandora" (Sussman 1978, 37),
though the specific relationships between changes in farming
techniques, economic decline, and this "virulent sexism" are
difficult to recover. Even more important than its sources,
however, are the echoes of Hesiod's sexism that are omni-
present in Greek literature and in the sphere of its influence.
The exclusion of the female from the world of discourse in
Hesiod constitutes, along with the degradation of the female
into a series of bestial grotesques in the poetry of Semonides
of Amorgos, the principal archaic manifestation of a hostility
that is one of the most problematic aspects of the subsequent
tradition.

The end of the *Theogony*, if we read it honestly in our own
historical moment, leaves us with deep contradictions. We
have here a body of archaic Greek poetry refreshingly free of
the otherwise pervasive proaristocratic bias. But in its representation of the sexes this poetry is both chilling and unset-
tling, laying bare a misogyny that, though it can be heard at
times in Homer as well, is here so fundamental a given of
this poetry that we can scarcely imagine a recognizable Hesiod without it.

But if Hesiod betrays entrenched social attitudes that we
find difficult to reconcile and impossible to endorse, we
should remember that these attitudes have emerged here incidentally, in a context from which they are at least superficially divorced. By contrast, to the extent that this poetry
answers the questions that it seems to invite us to ask, its
solutions are both startling and awe-inspiring.

The *Theogony* claims, first of all, to be about gods; secondarily, it is a poem about gods and men. These are the
primary concerns, and their resolution has been seen to be in
the form of a massive assertion of the humanizing power of

poetry. It is difficult to be specific concerning the relationship of the poem to the scattered and varied cults of archaic Greece, but it has rightly been emphasized that the Homeric and Hesiodic poems seem to have taken on something like the shapes in which we know them during the period of the rapid development of major Panhellenic institutions such as Delphi and Olympia. In a sense this poetry clearly sets out to reconcile and set in order the rights and prerogatives of all the gods the various Greek cities acknowledged in cult (along with others who never had cults).

It is the final irony of this self-denigrating speaker that the scale of his pretension (and of his accomplishment) as a poet turns out to be as sublime as his declared perspective is humble, and it is in that tension that much of his enduring attraction lies. The voice of the least of men, the most socially marginal of men, asserts its authority to describe a universe of which he, his perspective, his voice constitute both the center and the shaping principle.

III THE WORKS
AND DAYS

THE *WORKS AND DAYS* IS A POEM OF CONTRASTS, OF COLORFUL
and often discordant juxtapositions. Its sometimes unappar-
ent unity is a dramatic unity, orchestrated around a dramatic
situation, presumably fictional, but the traditional material
that makes up its bulk is rich in the binary oppositions dear
to the followers of Claude Lévi-Strauss. It is tempting to read
this poem as a structuralist of that school (whose interpretive
techniques strike an interesting harmony with the concerns
of ancient Pythagoreanism), insisting that these juxtapositions, these opposites, easily arranged into columns, are the
heart of the poem, its attraction and its reason for being. Thus
when the poet begins by dividing what is designated by *eris*
("strife") into two contrasting elements that we may label
"competition" and "contentiousness," he has elevated to the
level of a rhetorical and compositional principle this underlying predilection for binary oppositions preexisting in the
traditional material he is conveying. Prominent among these
is the concern, so extraordinarily widespread that it is a virtual universal of folk culture, with the pair nature/culture. We
can point to specific passages (such as the fable of the nightingale and the hawk, taken along with its delayed interpretation) that turn on this contrast, but more important is its
latent presence throughout as a shaping concern. Work and
idleness, justice and crime are similar pairs that surface only
periodically as explicit matters for discussion yet never quite
pass beyond the limits of consciousness.

Although the *Theogony* prooimion is the most important
passage for the development of the shepherd-of-Helikon persona, the *Works and Days* is the poem that insists on the individuality of the poet, his personal and idiosyncratic view of
the world and the highly specific conditions of his life. At the
same time, it is a poem whose content is traditional in the
most conspicuous way—it contains two long strings of proverbs and a beast fable, conveys conventional farming and seafaring lore that the poet explicitly derives from tradition, not
experience, and ends with a list of good-luck and bad-luck
days, a category of information at the farthest remove from
the personal or idiosyncratic. If this persona is so highly developed, part of the explanation is that the poem plays off the
highly individualized speaker against the highly generalized
content, and the effect is powerful. This speaker deprecates
himself and his addressee, Perses. They are peasants, and on
top of that they are parties in a petty squabble, pitted one
against the other in needless conflict over a miserable agricultural holding. But what the speaker has to say is vast,
infinitely removed from the muddled sphere of our misdi-
rected strivings against each other and against a reluctant and
impoverished world. The content is global, in touch with the
principle of Justice itself, with the gods and the relations of
gods and men, in touch, finally, with a vision of a society
ruled by justice, of what the world *could* be. It is hard to find
a modern analogy, but perhaps the closest is the works of
Ezra Pound, especially *The Pisan Cantos*, where the personal
and the universal are insistently juxtaposed in an analogous
way.

The short prooimion (1–10) initiates this contrast, as well
as other central contrasts, in a passage of extraordinary vir-
tuosity that in the range of archaic hexameter poetry marks
an extreme limit of ornamental contrivance. It is often said

that ancient Greek poetry is innocent of rhyme. The claim is
in any case untrue, since rhyme (and especially the weak
echoing of similar endings called *homoioteleuton*) is reasonably
frequent even in Homer, but it is true that rhyme is not (as it
is in English poetry) one of the formal elements that may
distinguish poetry from prose. It is very striking, however,
that in the ten verses of the prooimion we find not only three
rhymed couplets but pervasive internal rhymes as well, often
underlining balanced contrasts of sense. Beyond these un-
usual formal characteristics, the prooimion can be seen as a
subtle and idiosyncratic variant on the most characteristically
oral compositional feature of archaic Greek poetry, the ring.
The progression here is as follows:

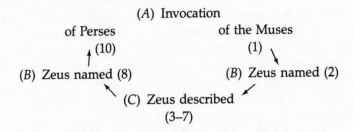

True, the statement of intent to lecture Perses is not a direct
address like that to the Muses, but it clearly corresponds to
that invocation in framing the description of Zeus. The effect
is bathetic. The very great, the universal, is balanced by the
very small, the personal, and specifically by the evocation of
an individual who will be treated with contempt. The list of
the powers of Zeus is a fabric of colorful paradoxes in which
the god's power over the affairs of men and the poet's power
over language are explicitly identified with one another. In a
series of variations on the ways in which Zeus increases and
decreases, exalts and debases, we are told first of all that he

makes men "unspoken of or praised / famous or unsung" (*aphatoi te phatoi te / rhetoi t' arrhetoi te*, 3–4). This is said to come about through Zeus's will, but of course the unspecified agents of the fame and praise are the poets, as all the speech-related verbal adjectives hint. The fifth line describes the world and itself, Zeus and its speaker, simultaneously:

> Easily he makes things grow [*briaei*], easily crushes
> what has grown big.

The balance of the two statements in the verse reproduces the so-called "thought rhythm" of Semitic poetry in a manner characteristic of much of the Hesiodic wisdom poetry (though whatever connection may exist between the *Works and Days* and the material preserved in Proverbs is beyond our ability to recover and trace). Embedded in the balanced statement here is a playful and self-conscious formal detail that shapes the richly worked language. The first syllable of the word "easily" (*rhea*), the repeated pivot of the thought of the line, changes in metrical value from the first to the third foot . . . the poet easily expands it and easily contracts it, exercising the control Zeus exercises over human affairs.

Throughout this talk of expanding and contracting, strengthening and weakening, the subject is clearly man, but the latent metaphor throughout these expandings and con-tractings is agricultural. The first verb in the line quoted above (briaei) is rare, but it also occurs in the *Theogony* (447), where it refers to what Hekate does to the flocks—she causes them to increase. Thus the prooimion by its language establishes a connection between Zeus's impact on human affairs and the influence of the forces of the natural world (including Hekate as the moon) on agricultural prosperity. Zeus strengthens, frustrates, diminishes, increases, straightens, and finally withers man, and behind that statement the choice of verbs repeatedly reminds us of the way the moon, planets, and seasons affect the productivity of the earth and agricultural wealth. The association of the agricultural calendar with justice is thus announced from the start, along with the peculiar Hesiodic insistence on the juxtaposition of the global and the specific, and the characteristically self-conscious Hesiodic problematics of language.

Enough has already been said about the violence we do these poems by imposing on them descriptive tables of contents that subordinate one section to another with misleading decisiveness and clarity. Still, given the confusing organization of the *Works and Days*, it seems essential to distinguish at least major sections in order to appreciate at once their independence and their interrelatedness.

1–10   prooimion
11–26   the "two strifes" (competition and conflict)
27–41   address to Perses: work! don't watch lawsuits!
42–105   Prometheus/Pandora
106–201   the five ages
    174–201   criticism of the present (iron) age
202–85   the fable and injunctions to Perses and the kings
    202–12   the fable
    213–24   injunction to Perses on Justice
    225–47   the city ruled by law and the city ruled by crime
    248–73   injunction to the kings on justice
    274–85   the fable interpreted
286–828   various advice to Perses
    286–326   praise of work
    327–41   treat others fairly and sacrifice to the gods
    342–80   proverbs
    381–617   the agricultural year

Some major shifts and movements within the poem appear immediately. The traditional title itself points to the problem—a title not attested before the second century of our era, though it may be a great deal older than that (West 1978, 136). The two elements of the title refer most obviously to discrete passages within the poem. The *Works* (*erga*) are the instructions on the various tasks of the agricultural year (381–617).

We might stretch the designation to include the instructions on seafaring attached to the agricultural lore (618–94), but the transition between the two sections is nevertheless clear. The *Days* (*hemerai*) are certainly the closing section (765–828) on lucky and unlucky days. The title thus seems to designate a provisional composite, but many more elements are actually present than those designated, and the solution of setting a limit at line 764 and declaring everything up to that point the *Works* (to the exclusion of the *Days*) proves unsatisfactory. In fact, the highly developed persona is explicitly stringing together a composite performance consisting of a variety of parts. Transitions such as line 106:

If you like, I'll run through another story . . .

emphasize the provisional quality of this particular performance and the speaker's power to pick and choose from an implied range of set pieces that vastly exceeds what he actually gives us here. Stand-up comedians use exactly the same technique. It is an enhancement of their power over us, a feigned indifference that is part of the act. But it does reveal at least what the speaker *wants* us to think of the organization of this poem. Any organic or necessary organization of the parts is explicitly denied and their provisional configuration expressed as a function of the choice—the explicitly free and arbitrary choice—of a highly individualized speaker, an identity in striking contrast to the impersonal and traditional nature of the information conveyed.

What the speaker in fact gives us is a long, somewhat rambling poem of advice and exhortation (286–828), prefaced by a far more complex sequence of myths, fables, and other traditional lore organized around the conflicts of a domestic lawsuit. The autobiographical material is essential to the opening section but penetrates the poem of advice explicitly only in the peculiar section on seafaring. The earlier part of the poem is organized as a justification and dramatic frame for the traditional wisdom imparted in the last 550 lines. There, the audience increasingly replaces the fading Perses, who, after all, has turned out simply to represent the ideal (mute) listener. What he is exhorted to lend ear to is in fact information directed at *us*, as the ideal audience. The organization of the earlier section is nevertheless fascinating, and it is here that the most memorable Hesiodic lore is found. One often has the sense that a set piece is being incorporated virtually without adaptation to the environment of this highly specific argument, with the result that the ubiquitous contrast of the individual with the general or paradigmatic impresses itself on our consciousness here as well.

The passage on the two Strifes (11–26) springs out of a void. Why does Perses need to hear these particular "true things" (*etetuma*, from the prooimion, 10)? To our ears, the cracker-barrel sociology inevitably smacks of a Darwinian "magic of the marketplace" in its glorification of competition as an essential component of human society, though, in fact, if reduced to a descriptive paradigm, it bears more resemblance to the economist Thorstein Veblen's "doctrine of emulation." We see what our neighbor has, and we want to have it, too, with the result that we work hard to compete and in the process ape the lifestyles of those more successful than ourselves. This is the thrust of the Hesiodic sociology. Even if his sympathies are with the victims of power, this Helikonian hayseed is no revolutionary. The first Strife, competition, glues society together and improves everyone's lot. The other Strife is destructive contentiousness, which has the opposite effect. At one extreme she is war, at the other, the squabbles of the law court. This Strife is the daughter of Night and mother of a host of evils described in the *Theogony* (225–32).

This is the Strife imposed on us by the malicious "will of the gods," with the result that we must honor her even though we hate her. The other strife (competition) is likewise a daughter of Night—a double of the original Strife—but in the distribution of honors Zeus has made her a benefit to mankind. Much of the theological strategy of the *Works and Days* is here already. The pantheon is essentially self-seeking and misanthropic and increasingly to be identified with the wretched "way-things-are." But the role of Zeus changes subtly—Zeus who has already been identified with the voice of the poet himself. We are beginning to see another side of Greek theological poetry.

Let us back away for a moment here and try to define the possibilities from a new perspective. I take it that when Greek poets speak of the gods they speak in some sense symbolically. That is to say that the gods of cult, the gods that demand certain formal acknowledgments and gestures of respect in the festivals, are only marginally implicated, if indeed they are implicated at all. The independent *existence* of the gods may have a meaning in terms of popular piety (or, more likely still, in terms of civic piety), but we have seen that in the Greek *Theogony*, poetry claims the right to create and destroy deities and remains aloof from the exploitative canonizations of cult. These gods exist, then, only as a function of the poetry that talks about them, and as such they have a certain representative or symbolic value within that poetry that is a function of its internal order and not imposed from outside. In the *Theogony*, the gods are representative of an order of the universe that is fundamentally hostile to the interests of man. Or, we might say, the gods are projections of *the-way-things-are*, and things are, finally, awful. Here in the opening of the *Works and Days* a new mode of utilization of these god-symbols seems to be emerging against the back-

drop of the one just described. The "will of the gods" (16) is
still that we live in Hell and thank them for the privilege. But
there is also the second Strife, competition, placed among us
by Zeus and *for our benefit* (18–19). In other words, theological
poetry can also use these god-symbols to represent the way
the world *could* be. The two modes correspond roughly to
tragedy (which takes the horror of the human condition as
the given and projects a divine apparatus to explain that condition) and comedy (which projects visions of a better world
and manipulates its symbols accordingly). This rough model
is not intended specifically to account for Attic drama. There,
we would need a third sort of utilization of these symbols—
the gods as projections of our *deluded fantasies* of the way
things are—to approach an adequate account. But the two
most fundamental modes of Greek poetry's theological account of the world seem to grow out of the Hesiodic tradition—the gods as symbols of *things-as-they-are* and the gods
as symbols of *things-as-they-could-be*. To the first corresponds
a pessimism close to paranoia that is the natural and general
effect of life in the world. To the second corresponds a hard-
won and tough-minded meliorism that projects the possibility
that (using what this poetry claims to be able to teach us) we
might be able to make that life better.

But again—why does Perses need to hear this discourse
on the two Strifes? Apparently it is because he has a tendency
to hang around the marketplace listening to the arguments in
the law courts. (Where are we, anyway, Askra or Athens?
Here again we see emerging a theme more familiar in its
Aristophanic form.) Perses is attracted to the wrong Strife,
the one that "delights in evil" (28). He is enjoined (in a mode
that will become all too familiar) to redirect his attention to
filling his stores with grain. Then comes one of the wrenching
transitions so characteristic of the corpus (35). Perses, it

seems, does not just listen to lawsuits—his more important failing is that he engaged in one with the speaker (who would like it reopened) and *won* by bribing the "kings" who sat in judgment. This is at once one of the most satisfying and most shocking moments in the corpus. You cannot imagine the Homeric narrator, who in comparison with Hesiod is a pious apologist for power, calling kings "bribe-eaters" and "suckers" (generally a good English equivalent for *nepioi*, which refers either to suckling infants or to those easily deluded). Homer will show us kings calling each other names and getting away with it (*Il.* 1.149, 225–32) or unworthy rabble-rousers doing the same thing and getting whipped for it (*Il.* 2.225–42), but his values in the situation are clear and traditional. The kings are right and will prevail, and the rabble are wrong and will be kept in line—strife among kings is the only thing to fear. Hesiodic values are vastly more sympathetic—more "modern" if you like. His espousal of the victim's perspective is one of the great surprises of archaic Greek literature.

What follows is not a development from this outburst regarding the unfair settlement of the lawsuit but a mythic elaboration on the realities lying behind the earlier injunction to fill the stores with grain. The point of departure is the line singled out earlier as emblematic of the Hesiodic account of the human condition and the implication of the gods in the failure of the world.

> The gods have hidden man's livelihood and keep it
> hidden.
>
> [42]

And it is not just "the gods" who are implicated here but specifically Zeus (47), who has now clearly slipped back among the symbols of *things-as-they-are*.

The *aition*—the explanation of the cause of the situation—

takes the form of the Prometheus/Pandora myth, discussed above, which most readers have felt appears in more developed form here than in the *Theogony*. The gods have given us this miserably inadequate existence out of spite because Prometheus cheated Zeus (and in this version it is unambiguous that he really *did* cheat him). This is a Zeus whose sadistic laughter (59) links him to his rough grandparents, who delighted in their mutual brutalities (*Theog.* 158, 173). The characteristics of Pandora—now named, and with bitter sarcasm (81)—are elaborated in great detail. The study remains to be written that will fully explore the implications of this bitter revenge (= woman) of the-way-things-are (= Zeus) perpetrated on the unbridled and exclusive male fantasy of the way things could be.

This, in any case, is Hesiod's first account of the world's failure, of which woman is both the agent (in opening the jar) and the embodiment (in the inherent "terrible lust," "limb-gnawing sorrows," "bitch mind," and "thieving character" all present in *her*, not in the jar [66–67]). The second is the myth of the five ages of man, an account that emphasizes the determinative effect of an inherent tendency in human history toward deterioration—in effect, the archaic, mythic expression of what Karl Popper isolated as Platonic historicism. That the myth is "historicist" in that it postulates a normal succession, a direction, in human history is beyond question, though it should be said that in this sense historicism is undoubtedly a general characteristic of mythic accounts of human development. There remains some doubt, however, whether its historicism is linear (and therefore ultimately pessimistic) or cyclical, based on the model of an endless and ultimately neutral succession of states of human experience oscillating from best to worst and then back again to best. It is undeniable that the opening lines of the description of the present (iron) age,

> I wish I were not among the fifth race of men,
> but either had died earlier or been born later
>
> [174–75]

seem to say that the present age is the nadir of a cycle, bracketed by better times. This interpretation is attractive from a number of points of view, not least because it would associate this Hesiodic account with a large class of mythic accounts of history characterized by periodicity and cyclical patterns. There is nevertheless an apparent contradiction here between the myth of cyclical development suggested by the lines quoted above and the rhetorical surface of the rest of the poem. The speaker is manifestly and habitually pessimistic. He degrades the present age just as he degrades himself, his interlocutor, and his community. This attitude is an essential one in the repertory of poses that constitute the Hesiodic persona. A cyclical account of human history may well be dimly perceptible beyond Hesiod's negative historicism, but the two verses quoted may just as easily be understood as a traditional and formulaic element in this particular Hesiodic routine, an elaborated poetic variant on the theme "Anything would be better than this!"

The cyclical pattern in history is not the only one that has been perceived as underlying the Hesiodic myth. Jean-Pierre Vernant (1983), has demonstrated the coherence of the scheme (in spite of certain apparent internal inconsistencies, discussed below) as a tripartite structure corresponding to the archetypal triad of Indo-European socioreligious thought explored by Georges Dumézil. Vernant sees the gold and silver ages, taken together, as corresponding to the religious and

judicial functions of kingship, the bronze and heroic ages to
the military function, and the current iron age to the function
of maintenance of fertility—an age of farmers, of peasants,
"mere stomachs." He likewise explores the relationship of
these three strata to youth, middle age, and old age. Again,
this analysis is highly suggestive and underlines the paradoxical relationship to tradition of this apparently idiosyncratic
poem.

Keeping both models in mind, let us take a look at the
myth as it unfolds in the poem. All interpreters agree that the
account of the ages of man demonstrates symptoms of the
adaptation and reconciliation of several levels of traditional
material. The gold-silver-bronze-iron scheme is discrete and
self-contained, but even here we can find evidence of internal
inconsistency. Once upon a time, in the reign of Kronos
(whom the Romans were to replace with Saturn), men lived
like gods, the earth produced grain spontaneously, old age
and misery were unknown, and men simply fell asleep when
their time came. The men of this golden age became *daimones*—the idea of daimones ("lower divinities," hence "de-
mons") as a rank of beings intermediate between gods and
men is good Hesiodic lore—and were replaced by a race of
men each of whom remained in a state of infancy for a century, followed by a short adulthood made miserable by their
disorderly passions. They failed to sacrifice to the gods and
so were shoveled under by Zeus, although they still have
honor down below. After this silver age came one with bronze
houses and walls, and the first warriors, but ignorant of iron.
What has happened here? The first two metals were purely
symbolic: gold is best, silver next best. But now the bronze
and iron ages seem to be based on the availability of technology (however fancifully represented) and thus to correspond to the periods of the modern scheme of prehistory.

Even more suggestive than the mixing of the two modes of signification in the list of metals is the perception that bronze technology preceded iron technology historically. This is of course accurate, but how could this tradition of poetry *know* that it was accurate? I assume that it could not. The available information is the information before us, but at some point in its unrecoverable history this purely symbolic schema of human development incorporated information corresponding to the recoverable facts of technological development. A comparable encoding of the same development can be found in Homer, where the references to iron are few and some at least are probably anachronisms. What is surprising, though, is that there are not more anachronisms and that the technology available at the time of the telling is not projected back into the ancient story.

The metal-age scheme is interrupted at this point by the seemingly incongruous age of the heroes. No mystery, however, surrounds the source of this apparent reversal of the downward movement of history. It is simply a mutual accommodation of two prevalent modes of pessimistic historicism, the Hesiodic and another that we may call Homeric. The age of the heroes is a literary age, the projection back into mythified history of the epic tradition, which itself represents the heroes of the past as bigger and better than the men of today. The epicycle, the upturn in human events, is only apparent. If the heroes are "better and more just" (158), the thrust of tradition is that they are so in comparison with *ourselves*, not with their predecessors. In any case, they have all gone (as in Homer, only Menelaus is destined to go) to the isles of the blessed and have left this diminishing world to the wretched men of our own time. Rather than describe this fallen state in detail, the speaker immediately shifts to the prophetic future tense, projecting the closest thing to a last judgment one can imagine in a tradition whose gods are essentially indifferent to the moral state of mankind.

What is sketched is a total breakdown of ethical order, the failure of all bonds of obligation, family, and friendship, terminal alienation from the gods, the victory of evil over good, and the entire replacement of justice (*dike*) by force. This will be the final victory of the evil Strife of lines 14–16, signaled by the departure for Olympos of Aidos ("Respect") and Nemesis (usually thought of as "Retribution," but Lattimore nicely translates "Decency" here). And how will the end come?

> What will be left for mortal men
> will be bitter pain. There will be no defense against
> evil.
>
> [200–201]

That is, we will take care of the details of our destruction ourselves. Why should the gods bother? Our destruction will be the result of our own natural inclinations, untempered by any value capable of restraining our lust for immediate gratification. The humanism of this prophecy is both implicating and disturbing, vastly more so than the infantile and paranoid threats of divine retribution with which the prophetic literatures of the ancient world and the modern are strewn. Hesiod on this subject is as disillusioned and immediate as today's paper.

After the account of the ages of man comes a new transition, again marked by an explicitly arbitrary decision of the speaker: "Now I'll tell a fable" (*ainos*, 202). This word is an interesting one and deserves a place alongside *kleos* (fame) among the words through which early hexameter poetry designates itself and its strategies. An ainos is essentially a story told for an ulterior motive, a motive that does not appear on the surface. The most frequent and characteristic form such storytelling takes is the beast fable, and this particular ainos belongs in that category, but in the *Odyssey* (14.508) the word refers to Odysseus's false tale told to Eumaios to hint that he needs a coat. The essential factor, then, is a multiplicity of levels of meaning, such as always characterizes beast fables, and a parallel deviousness of intention on the part of the storyteller. By way of the related *ainigma* (enigma, riddle) we reach the vocabulary used in the Ps.-Platonic *Second Alcibiades* (147b) to characterize *all* poetry, *ainigmatodes*, "enigmatic, riddling, obscure." Finally, the related verb *ainittomai* (to say cryptically, hint) is the principal tool of the Greek language throughout antiquity to designate secondary or multiple levels of meaning in texts and myths.

An ainos requires interpretation (just as a beast fable is normally accompanied by a moral tag), but here the narrative voice makes us wait for that interpretation. The fable itself floats luminously before the mind's eye for sixty lines before the speaker tells us what it means, and by that time it already has many provisional meanings, since it is the nature of fables to implicate their audience in the creation of their meaning by their very resistance to interpretation. The fable itself is simple and easily paraphrased: a hawk ($\male$) takes a nightingale ($\female$), who pleads for her life. The hawk's answer is a chilling evocation of the characteristic discourse of the wielders of power from the Melian dialogue of Thucydides to the present. The essential reality is power. The hawk can have the nightingale for lunch or let her go. Protest is futile. The point is summed up in what is clearly a proverbial tag:

> Whoever opposes those more powerful is a fool.
>
> [210]

The fable has been explicitly addressed to the kings (202), but as soon as it is finished, the speaker turns to Perses (213) to enjoin him to justice (*dike*) over crime (*hubris*). But this seems initially at odds with what has gone before. In a beast fable, the talking animals represent people, the fable itself, some human situation. This fable seems to make the point that right is a function of might and human relations are governed by unmediated force. It is simply the way of the world that the strong have the weak for lunch. If that is the case, then why all this fuss about justice and crime? The new outburst against the "bribe-eaters" (221) and the perversion of justice seems to have forgotten the apparent lesson of the fable, since at this point we are likely, if we are thoughtful, to have lit on one of the traditional decipherings of the riddle: the nightingale (literally, the "singer") = Hesiod and the hawk = the kings. Nevertheless, the speaker rises to a new pitch of rhetoric in his praise of justice as a principle of conduct, including portraits of two cities, the one ruled by justice (and therefore peaceful, self-sustaining, fertile, orderly), the other by crime (and so sterile, doomed to destruction).

As addressed to Perses and to society as a whole, this praise of justice over crime has emphasized the way in which these qualities are infused into the community, and it is already clear that they originate in one man or at most a few men. When the speaker turns to the kings (248), the emphasis shifts to Zeus (once again *things-as-they-could-be*) as overseer of justice—in fact, as the father of Justice, a relationship confirmed in a richly allegorizing section of the *Theogony* (902). The powerful, in other words, will determine whether justice or crime will rule a community. And since the powerful have a natural affinity for crime, some higher force is required to keep them honest so that the community may be saved. It is important to remember that it is in this context that a providential, justice-favoring Zeus emerges in this poem, and so in Greek theology. The poet claims a power that goes beyond the power of kings—the power to shape and articulate the very nature of reality. He is pitted here against the real and immediate power relationships of society, and his recourse (as a victim, a have-not, in this arena) is to postulate an order of the world that limits the power of the powerful. The tone modulates again (and again echoes a characteristic prophetic mode):

> Remember this, kings, and talk straight,
> you bribe-eaters, and forget about crooked judgments.
>
> [263–64]

It is as if the poet now had a power on his own side that made him able to stand up to corrupt force, the power of a justice that is his own creation and that his voice has woven into the fabric of the world. The proverbial expression of the resultant situation brings us as close as this poetry will come to a poetry of divine retribution:

> The man who does evil to another does evil to himself,
> and bad counsel is worst for the giver.
>
> [265–66]

The section ends with a coda (267–73), in which the speaker says that he would raise his son to be a criminal (since criminality is so clearly rewarded in society) were it not that he believes that Zeus ultimately favors justice. Once again, the idea is one most familiar from comedy. The dilemma is that of Strepsiades in the *Clouds*, and it is the core of Khremylos's question to the oracle in the *Ploutos*. A painfully immediate aspect of the problem of justice is opened up here. In a world where success is closely linked to corruption, should we raise our children to be corrupt successes or honest victims of the successful tactics of the corrupt? The only alternative is to remake the world—and that, finally, is the implicit project of this poetry.

We are far from the ainos, but the necessary interpretation is finally before us. The fable turns out to have been exploited in a highly innovative way in this poem. Its system of signification is far more complex than the Hesiod = nightingale interpretation suggested, though such provisional formulations are never entirely lost, and Hesiod's explanation of the fable is not an exclusive closure. In fact, the hawk is a hawk and the nightingale a nightingale! The fable, which by the conventions of its genre should cryptically represent a situation in the human world, in fact expresses a truth about the specifically nonhuman world of nature. It is a *false* representation of the world of human experience, because justice is a real (or at least realizable) factor in the latter:

> Perses . . . respect justice and abandon force!
> This is the law Zeus has set for men.
> For fish and beasts and winged birds, the law is
> that they eat each other, since there is no justice among
>   them.
> But to men, he gave justice, which is much better.
>
>   [274–81]

The divorce is complete. On one side, the natural world, whose failure to sustain us is linked to the perverse deities representing *things-as-they-are* and whose only values are those stemming from the immediate gratification of the desires of the powerful. On the other, the human universe, which *can* be ruled by justice, whose symbol is Zeus, now fully transformed into a poetic symbol of *things-as-they-could-be*.

What follows in the bulk of the poem is advice about how to live in this world, a fallen and fundamentally alien environment in which we can survive as humans only in the protective bubble of that which finally defines us as human: our own creation, justice. The introductory section, in its rambling yet deliberate way, has drawn together culture, the male, work, justice, Zeus, poetry, and the interests of the victims, to oppose to them nature, the female, idleness, crime, the gods of traditional theology, the crooked language of power, and the interests of the powerful. The overriding and unifying statement is an assertion of the power of poetry and its allies over the enemy camp.

At this point, the essential system of values of the *Works and Days* has already been blocked out. Much of what follows focuses on the pair work/idleness and takes the form of injunctions to Perses to focus his energies and so ensure his survival.

The entire exposition is bound up in a further opposition developed in the latter part of the poem—the paradoxical valuation of knowledge (conceived as truth derived from tradition) over experience. The injunction to Perses to choose justice over crime contained the striking observation that "even a sucker learns from experience" (218). Injunctions to accept (the speaker's) good counsel reinforce this position (293–97), culminating in the speaker's ironic presentation of his own credentials to deliver useful information on seafaring (646–62). It is better to accept the bard's privileged lesson, formulated out of tradition and thus itself constituting an element of the protective bubble of humanity, than to muddle around in a basically hostile and dangerous environment. Experience is the worst source of knowledge, simply because it is a slow route and entails unnecessary risk.

This is a peculiar complex of ideas. First and most obviously, the bard as mouthpiece for the traditional wisdom is asserting his power and establishing the validity of that power. Don't bother trying to figure it out yourself, he says. Just listen to me and I'll tell you how to get things done—not, of course, because I have personal experience of these things, but because I am a bard (and so embody the traditional lore, the gift of the Muses).

This poetry's assertion of its ability to humanize the universe is here in the process of creating the conditions for its own exposure as hubristic (that is, as promising more than it can deliver). Though its characteristic discourse is that of the *eiron,* the self-deprecating understater, it can also play at being an *alazon,* an overreacher who asserts a claim to knowledge beyond his or her experience. The speaker even anticipates that exposure and plays with the outrageous consequences of his claims. Plato's *Ion* is the canonical demonstration of the completion of the process, the exposure of the bearer of the tradition as a bearer of empty words, with no real understanding of the subjects he describes so movingly. The assault there is primarily on Homer as authority, but if Hesiod has any immunity to such attack, it is only because his elusive ironies already contain its seeds.

Much of the information conveyed takes the form of short, proverbial (or gnomic) utterances. Some are extraordinarily abrupt and primitive in form. For all its awkwardness, the following is a fair literal translation of line 354:

> Both give, whoever gives, and don't give, whoever
> doesn't give.

The point is that generosity should be limited to those who reciprocate, but the expected syntactical relationships are not expressed, and the abruptness is felt even more acutely in the Greek original than in this English version. This proverbial sentence clearly depends heavily on the inflection of the speaker for intelligibility, and it is surely among the crudest and least literary utterances preserved in the corpus of Greek literature.

At the other extreme, in the account of the seasons of the agricultural year, this encyclopedic lore is expanded and elaborated in passages of exceptional beauty. Perhaps the richest of these is the description of the dog days of late summer (582–96), where many of the characteristic Hesiodic notes are sounded in an evocation of the pastoral landscape that was to be echoed in Hellenistic poetry:

When the thistle is in bloom and the droning cicada
clings to the tree and pours down the shrill, persistent
　　song
from his wings, in the sweltering season that drains the
　　strength—
that is when the goats are fattest and the wine is best
when women are most lecherous and men most
　　impotent,
since the Dog Star sears the head and knees
and the skin is dry and burnt. Then
we must have rocky shade and Thracian wine,
the best bread and the last milk the goats will give,
with the meat of a heifer that grazed in the forest
and of firstborn kids. Then drink the bright wine
while you sit in the shade after eating your fill,
and turning your face to the fresh west wind,
pour three libations of water from the unfailing spring
that pours down—the clear one—
and pour the fourth libation of wine.

This landscape (like that of later pastoral) has multiple aspects. It can be a sustaining and comfortable environment or a hostile and destructive one. The side of nature that we see here is near the latter extreme, and what strikes us most forcibly is the devaluation of the natural landscape, the alienation of the farmer from the land that reluctantly sustains him and the hostility of the destructive cosmic powers that preside over it. The "droning cicada" (*ekheta tettinks*) is a fixture of the conventional pastoral landscape and has generally positive associations. These are spelled out in Sokrates' praise of the sound in the *Phaedrus* (230c). But even if the praise of the cicada by poets and philosophers echoes this passage of Hesiod, the associations of the sound here are with the terrible heat of the sun and the deleterious effects of the Dog Star. The shrill buzz underscores and gives voice to the searing landscape. The abrupt transition in the middle of the passage is the key to the contrast being developed ("Then / we must have rocky shade . . ."). From a vision of a natural landscape that drains, sears, and emasculates, we pass into a sheltered and humanized world made possible by human effort, a world characterized by extraordinary abundance, some of it locally produced and some, notably, acquired by commerce. It is a refuge, from the Dog Star, first of all, but also from women, whose lust is represented as an exceptional threat at this brutal season. The ease of this retreat, its status as an emblem of the victory of (male) culture over the threatening aspect of man's environment, is summed up in the anonymous ritual prescribed in the final lines, the leisurely libations that either evoke the harmony of *this* existence with the powers that rule the universe or at the very least assert the possibility of keeping those powers at bay.

However hesitant we may be to believe that what Hesiod provides is an accurate account of the life of a particular Greek agricultural community at a specific moment in history, it should nevertheless be stressed that in peasant societies the continuities are extraordinary. To the extent that the conditions of farming conveyed here are reflected in the rhythm and activities of the agricultural year in the Mediterranean region today, we have good reason to believe that Hesiod's calendar corresponds to the realities of farming in preclassical Greece. The major technological advances in Greek agriculture belong largely to the generation since the Second World War, though the cultural and ethnic composition of the people of the Greek countryside has changed several times over. For much of the period from the Slavic invasions of the sixth and seventh centuries to the creation of an ethnic Greek state in the nineteenth, Hellenism was a largely urban phenomenon, and the peasants who worked the soil were commonly Slavs (or later Albanians), while high mountain pastures were exploited equally by nomadic non-Greek-speaking Vlachs and nomadic Greek-speaking Sarakatsans. The modern name of what we take to be Hesiod's Helikon, Zagaras, seems to be Slavic (cf. Russian *za gorye*, "by the mountain")—though the population that gave it that name is no longer in evidence. In spite of these changes, the correspondences are amazing, and, as suggested in chapter 1, there are many reasons why this poem's picture of the agricultural year seems to fit that of the valley of the Arkhontitsa today.

The general outline of Hesiod's agricultural year can be seen in the tabular outline offered earlier in this chapter. It is blocked out in terms of astronomical phenomena—the solstices and the heliacal risings of constellations and conspicuous stars—and the dates as reconstructed (West 1978, 252–53) correspond remarkably well to the modern rhythm of agriculture in central Greece. In fall, when the sap is down, you cut wood. Hesiod's farmer also has to worry about constructing his wooden plow, as did many successive generations. Plowing and seeding are done in the fall, since the growing season for grass (and so for grain) in the Mediterranean world is the winter, when there is adequate moisture. Not the cold of January and February—despite Hesiod's lamentations on the attendant miseries for man and beast—but rather the dessication of July and August is the obstacle to growing man's staple food. Therefore the land is plowed and the seed sown after the fall rains have softened the soil. Midwinter is then a time of idleness, a time to concentrate on protecting oneself from the wind and rain. This is when the fruits of summer foresight are reaped, the period the imprudent man will not survive. At the end of February (sixty days after the winter solstice), when Arcturus is an evening star, the swallows return and vines must be trimmed; then follows another lull until the harvest in May and June.

In fact (though Hesiod does not indicate it), these last are the months that threaten death by starvation, the time just before the new harvest when, though the weather is beautiful, supplies of grain are at their lowest level. Much of the history of Mediterranean agricultural economy is the history of the attempt to keep enough land in efficient grain production to provide reserves against the threat of spring starvation, a threat that is most acute, of course, the year following a bad harvest. The problem was not solved before the industrial revolution.

After the account of the harvest comes the passage just quoted. The brutal heat of July and August is again a time to take measures against the threat posed by a hostile world, but threshing and storing grain must also be dealt with. During this period, then as now (except where irrigation has changed old patterns), the vines are the principal productive plants, and the grapes have the peculiar virtue of ripening in the most intolerable season, when the rest of the landscape is parched and yellow-brown. After the September grape harvest and the preparation of the wine, the farmer again cuts his wood and waits for the fall rains to begin plowing.

Seafaring is an afterthought, and attempts to establish that a farmer from a dusty corner of Boeotia, hours from salt water, would in fact go off on commercial sailing ventures after the grain harvest are utterly unconvincing. This is information of another class, developed by and for a culture far from the valley of the Arkhontitsa. Predictably enough, the resultant passage is a mosaic of contradictory valuations and bizarre shifts of pose on the part of the narrator: Sailing is greedy, dangerous, and undesirable. Better not to do it at all. Our father did it, and look where *we* ended up! I've never done it (or almost never), but I'll tell you all about how to do it.

The value of the autobiographical information has already been discussed in evaluating the Hesiodic persona, and there is no need to reiterate here. Still, if there is in the entire corpus a set piece that cries out that it is an adaptation of ill-fitting material to a context which—whatever its claims—seems in fact to be the Helikonian festival of the Muses, this is it. When the Hesiodic voice wanders farthest from home, it protests most loudly that where it belongs is the precinct of the Muses in the valley of the Arkhontitsa.

Plutarch, who lived a few miles from the shrine and visited it, rejected much of the passage on seafaring, specifically the section in which Hesiod comically undermines his own credibility by telling the story of his unique sea voyage. Plutarch's comments reach us only by way of a paraphrase quoted by a scholiast, but the ancient scholar is unambiguous: "Plutarch says that all this about Khalkis and Amphidamas and the contest and the tripod has been interpolated, on the grounds that there is nothing sound in it." The scholiast goes

on to say that someone—almost certainly still Plutarch—
"calls all of this frivolous and takes up again at the lines about
the proper time for sailing [that is, at W&D 663]." That there
is a problem here seems to have been noticed well before
Plutarch, but the testimony of an exceptionally educated and
articulate local is of considerable value. Plutarch's reasons for
rejecting the passage were probably bound up in a desire to
reduce the text to that portion that was in his view ethically
and practically useful; he had little use for its ironies and coy
contradictions. But whatever his reasons for rejecting these
lines as "frivolous" interpolation, he must have known that
in so doing he was exposing as a fraud the Helikonian priests'
most prized treasure, the tripod that they showed visitors
(including Pausanias and no doubt Plutarch himself) as Hesiod's personal dedication. They claimed that this tripod had
been won by Hesiod in Euboea and thus was the very one
described in lines 656–59. Pausanias does not indicate that
they claimed the victory was over Homer, but they may well
have done so. That the contest of Homer and Hesiod was a
"late" accretion to the corpus is of course a commonplace,
and from antiquity attempts have been made to restore this
passage to exclude any hint of a reference to it. But if Hesiod
as we know him—the personal, confessional Hesiod—is a
function of the festival, rather than the reverse, the problem
disappears (see above, pp. 47–48). What better way for the
sponsors of this particular tradition of archaic poetry to assert
its supremacy over its rivals?

From this point on, the advice brought forward is rather
less organized, and a number of apparent contradictions
emerge. The advice on picking a wife (695–705) seems at odds
with line 406, where Perses is advised to get a servant woman
(emphatically *not* a wife) to take care of the house and do farm
work. But there is no real contradiction, and these lines are

entirely compatible with the observation at the end of the Pandora story in the *Theogony* that, bad as women are, they are the only means by which we can get (male) offspring, essential to ensure comfort and support in old age. The following string of proverbs (706–64) deals in large measure with sexual intercourse and fertility (as well as urination, an association that needs no comment). The final series of proverbs, a not inappropriate closing sequence, exhorts the listener to watch out for his reputation.

The final section on lucky and unlucky days (765–828) has found few admirers, and it is probably safe to say that few readers take the trouble to read it through. That is, whether these lines are in some sense integral to the poem or not, any modern audience for poetry of this sort finds them a quaint curiosity at best. Probably the best we can do is to try to think of them in the context of modern newspaper astrology columns. Both belong to a category of literature of great (if largely unexplored) importance, the prime function of which is to link the details of everyday life to cosmic principles of order. It is easier to live in the kind of world this information shapes. One is made to feel at home in a universe that, if it is not exactly favorable to our interests, at least leaves open the possibility of adapting our actions to its arbitrary fluctuations by means of this privileged information. It projects, in other words, the possibility of using what passes as age-old wisdom to make our life in this world less intolerable. And that, after all, is the central claim that the *Works and Days* makes for the tradition it represents.

IV THE OTHER HESIODS

THE TWO POEMS THAT HAVE OCCUPIED OUR ATTENTION TO THIS point form the heart of the Hesiodic corpus, the essential Hesiod. As the recently discovered poem that serves as epigraph to this volume shows, poets continued to sing through the mask of the shepherd of Mount Helikon well into Roman times, though that little poem can hardly be considered an attempt to enlarge the Hesiodic corpus. A considerable body of earlier poetry—in general datable only as pre-Hellenistic, since the first evidence of its existence is commonly of Hellenistic date—did pass as Hesiod's, however, and all of this material cannot simply be shrugged off as a series of literary exercises in the manner of Hesiod. Its origins are far more complex than such a model would suggest, and there is every reason to believe that much of it is as old as or older than many lines that we grant without hesitation to "Hesiod."

We have already seen that the corpus was much larger in antiquity and contained a number of works that are now only names, with testimonia and in some case a few paltry fragments attached, as well as a few works that have fared better over time. The medieval manuscript tradition included only the poems already discussed, along with the *Shield of Herakles*, but the *Catalogue of Women* is reasonably well known through a substantial number of ancient papyri that have come to light in modern times. Of the poems that are for all practical purposes lost forever, a few have titles that suggest how they fit into the corpus and how they acquired their Hesiodic status.

It is clear, first of all, that the *Works and Days* was not the only wisdom poetry attributed to Hesiod. The poem entitled the *Precepts of Kheiron*, of which less than three lines survive, was apparently generally accepted as Hesiodic until Aristophanes of Byzantium—a voice to be reckoned with, since he is known to have edited the *Theogony*—denied the attribution sometime around 200 B.C. This is doubly interesting, first because it indicates that wisdom poetry of various sorts was considered Hesiodic, and second because this Hesiodic wisdom poetry could apparently speak through personae other than that of the shepherd of Helikon. One must assume that the centaur of Pelion spoke his "precepts" in his own voice and that he addressed them to his most famous pupil, Akhilleus, perhaps a mute persona on the model of Perses and Kyrnus. If poetry of advice tended to be thought of as Hesiodic, it is hardly surprising that archaic or archaizing hexameters about farming and astronomical lore flocked to the corpus as well. Thus we have some reason to believe that there was a longer version of the *Works* and a Hesiodic *Astronomy*, as well as the *Ornithomanteia*, or instructions on divination by observation of the flight of birds, which the speaker of the *Works and Days* seems to introduce at the end of that poem. A few scantily attested mythological poems (including the *Wedding of Keyx* and *Peirithous's Descent into Hades*) may well have been elaborations of sections of the *Catalogue of Women* of the same sort as the *Shield of Herakles*.

It is these last two poems, however, that will occupy us principally in our exploration of the variations on Hesiodic poses and themes that lie beyond the corpus, narrowly defined. Just as the *Works* seems to have had a double, called by a scholiast the *Great Works* and incorporating lines absent

from our received text of the canonical poem on agriculture,
so the *Catalogue* had a double, attested principally through
multiple citations in Pausanias and in various scholia and
known as the *Great Catalogue*. It is highly unlikely that the
longer forms of these poems constituted independent works.
Rather, they must have been versions that included lines and
passages that for one reason or another did not occur in versions that had become canonical. All evidence for the longer
forms of the poems, in any case, is Hellenistic or later and so
dates from a period when the Hellenistic scholars and the
expanded book trade may be thought of as having established
critical—or at least conservative—texts of each poem.

The *Catalogue of Women* may well be the best-preserved
"lost" poem of the ancient world, excepting only the plays of
Menander. This peculiarity of their transmission presumably
indicates that both the plays of Menander and the *Catalogue*
of Hesiod enjoyed a popularity in the Roman period that en-
sured their frequent copying and citation, but somehow that
popularity did not win them direct manuscript transmission.
The tradition is fickle, and the reasons for its loss of specific
works will always be uncertain, but in the case of the *Catalogue*
we may realistically conjecture a genuine fluctuation of critical
opinion. It was certainly a poem that was greatly appreciated
in the Hellenistic period for its antiquarian lore. This popularity clearly lasted well into Roman times, and all the great
libraries of the ancient world doubtless had copies down to
the time of their various destructions. But whether the last
copy went with the arrival of the Arabs in Alexandria in 642
or with that of the Franks in Constantinople in 1204, the *Catalogue* was not one of the works destined to be salvaged from
the wreckage by the Christian heirs of the ancient philological
tradition, for reasons that must have had to do with style as
well as content. Its rambling account of the aristocracy of a

dim past had little chance of surviving the last vestiges of concern for that aristocracy.

What is known of the broad lines of the *Catalogue* is summed up in the arrangement of the 262 fragments and testimonia collected by Merkelbach and West (see West 1985). Only a small part of this material is accessible in translation—indeed, since most of the fragments are preserved only on shreds of papyrus (with the result that we often have only the beginnings or the ends of the lines), restoration to the point where translation can produce satisfactory results poses almost insurmountable problems. It is nevertheless clear that the organization of the *Catalogue*, like a substantial amount of its content, was genealogical, and certain major sections can be blocked out, including the stories of the descendants of Aiolos, Inachos, and Pelasgos, the daughters of Atlas and their descendants, and the courtship of Helen. Some of the most substantial surviving fragments belong to this last section, including a reference to Akhilleus's education by Kheiron on Mount Pelion, which may have something to do with the attribution of the *Precepts* to Hesiod (fr. 204).

By far the best sample we have of the *Catalogue of Women*, however, is the opening section of the poem known as the *Shield of Herakles*, whose attribution to Hesiod was questioned in antiquity but which nevertheless remained attached to Hesiod's name and survives in the manuscript tradition both in isolation and in association with the *Works and Days* and the *Theogony*. The opening fifty-six lines of this poem may be taken to represent the section of the *Catalogue* that deals with Alkmene, the mother of Herakles. The story—most familiar in the form it takes in Plautus's *Amphitruo*—of Zeus's impersonation of Amphitryon to gain access to his wife, the cuckold's return to sleep with her on the same night, and the subsequent birth of twins, one far superior to the other (because his father was divine), is told here for the first time in surviving literature. Just how characteristic the passage might be of the *Catalogue* as a whole is difficult to say. It seems to be a relatively elaborate episode, incorporating some colorful details, but here, as presumably elsewhere, the narrative texture is thin and the ancient lore itself seems to justify the telling.

That Zeus should stop on Mount Phikion, a barren peak a few miles west of Thebes, as the last stage of his journey, after striding down the peaks from Olympos to climb into Alkmene's bed also imparts to the story a disorienting juxtaposition of human and divine scale and a sense of wonder that we have learned to associate with Hesiod. The Boeotian place-name Phikion also gives the story a little local color— as well as evoking the name Phiks (the Boeotian for "Sphinx") used in the *Theogony* (326) and generally said to be the unique instance of a specifically Boeotian dialect form in the language of the national poet of archaic Boeotia.

Beyond this introductory section representing the *Catalogue* entry, the *Shield* proper has found few admirers among modern readers (with the notable exception of Apostolos Athanassakis, whose introduction to his translation of the poem is both appreciative and sensitive). It is clearly a parasitic work, a narrative and descriptive expansion and stylistic tour de force easily separable from the text that serves as its pretext. The *Catalogue* by its very nature invites this sort of expansion of individual episodes, and the phenomenon we see here is undoubtedly repeated again and again in the history of archaic hexameter poetry, though the relationship of "original" and "secondary" material is seldom as clear-cut. The *Shield* (or something very much like it and going under the same name) is at least as old as the early sixth century, when Stesikhoros is said to have asserted that it was indeed an authentic poem of Hesiod. A Byzantine introduction to the poem provides the information that an Athenian named Megakleides asserted the poem's authenticity while underlining the absurdity of Hesiod's claim that Hephaistos should have made arms for Herakles, his mother's archenemy. In the Hellenistic period, Aristophanes of Byzantium is again credited with the exposure of this Hesiodic "fraud," and his judgment was apparently based on his accurate perception that the poem seems to derive from the Homeric description of the shield of Akhilleus (*Il.* 18.478–608). This argument from imitation no longer holds water now that we know a great deal more than any Alexandrian textual critic could have known of the nature of the traditions of Greek hexameter poetry and their interactions. Generally more interesting is the affirmation of the authenticity of the *Shield* by Apollonios of Rhodes (who must have been about forty years older than Aristophanes). Apollonios based his conclusion both on content (and the agreement of the *Shield* with the *Catalogue*) and, more important, on style (*kharakter*). Apollonios was certainly a good judge of hexameter poetry and the styles of its practitioners from its beginnings to his own time. If he read the *Shield* as Hesiodic in style, that is excellent testimony that it fell within the pale, within the possible range of variation of the Hesiodic corpus. Even if the best estimate of modern scholarship is right and the poem reflects the world of the early decades of the sixth century B.C., I for one see no contradiction and no reason either to doubt that the Hesiodic canon could still receive major additions at that date or to suggest that the *Shield* is any less Hesiodic for having reached its present form long after the death of the generation of bards in the main reponsible for our *Theogony* and *Works and Days*.

After the passage from the *Catalogue of Women* on Alkmene, the *Shield* sets out to tell the story of the duel in which

Herakles killed a Thessalian aristocrat named Kyknos (Swan).
The overall organization is a sufficient approximation of a
huge compositional ring to suggest that it is an authentic
product of the oral traditions of the Hesiodic bards. Whether
it is in fact an oral composition is unknowable and finally
irrelevant—much of the hexameter poetry that we take to be
of oral origin may in fact be literate imitation of the easily
aped oral style. The narrator goes abruptly from his account
of Alkmene to announce his new subject (57), introducing
Kyknos in close association with his father, Ares. After a con-
versation between Herakles and his charioteer and nephew,
Iolaos, we are given the conventional scene of the arming of
the hero, familiar from many Iliadic examples. The description
of the shield itself, the heart of the poem and the source of
its title, is framed by the arming scene and represents the
speaker's point of greatest departure from his pretext in the
Alkmene story (139–319). He then returns to the duel itself,
narrated in language of exceptional energy and rich orna-
ment. Once Kyknos is dead, Herakles must fight with Ares
(as we retrace the thematic sequence to its source, 424–62).
The ring is not closed—we never get back to the *Catalogue*—
and the final lines are a little ragged. We learn abruptly that
this Kyknos was hated by Apollo because he was in the habit
both of attacking pilgrims passing through Thessaly on their
way to Delphi and of stealing offerings meant for the god.
This sudden revelation has given the poem a political context
and a plausible date, but clearly much of the material is independent of this context, and the political message is, from
our perspective, hardly obtrusive.

The poem itself is of interest to us primarily as an extreme
example of the variety of hexameter styles that can be accom-
modated within the Hesiodic corpus. The language of the
Shield invites such adjectives as "baroque" or "mannerist."

Just as the overwhelming difference in taste and aesthetic thrust between the Homeric corpus and the Hellenistic *Argonautika* of Apollonios comes through loud and clear in translation, so this bizarre and aberrant archaic gem retains its individuality. The kind of thing the speaker of this poem does to excite us, to fill us with wonder, has an outrageousness about it that is both satisfying and liberating. It is almost as if we had taken a single step from the sober heroic battle narrative of Homer down the long road that connects it to such manifestations of the same Indo-European tradition as the extraordinary Irish epics—the *Táin Bó Cuailnge*, for example, with its infinitely greater imaginative range and tolerance for (or more accurately, cultivation of) exaggerations of preposterous scale.

Hesiod's *Shield* is about 50 percent longer than the description of the shield of Akhilleus in *Iliad* 18, the passage with which it most obviously invites comparison. While one is by no means a slavish imitation of the other, the difference in bulk nevertheless points to an important difference between the two texts, specifically the expansiveness of the Hesiodic text, its inclusiveness and elaboration. Both descriptions are episodic, broken into discrete accounts of the various scenes depicted on the respective artifacts, and both have a preference for narrative, readily elaborating static images into running stories that imply colorful movement. Hesiod is more schematic, proceeding explicitly from the central image, a serpent, to the rim, which, as on Akhilleus's shield, represents Okeanos. Some of the same motifs are there, including the city at war and the city at peace (with which the Homeric description opens and the Hesiodic one closes), the dance, and the lions attacking other beasts (the originals in archaic Greek art are so easily imagined). The two shields are similarly overloaded—each has approximately ten discrete scenes—and neither makes a serious claim to realism. Both, in other words, are explicitly exaggerations, heroic expansions describing bigger-than-life artifacts . . . the sort of armor the gods used to create for the heroes of the remote past.

Hesiod's description is characterized, however, by even greater exaggeration, even greater imaginative range. Let us look at a few sample lines. About the image of Perseus pursued by the sisters of Medusa and escaping by the use of his winged shoes we are told that he "was suspended [in the air] like a thought" (222), a simile whose daring juxtaposition of the archaic immediacy of the mythic scene with an extreme psychologizing abstraction is stunning. The idea is by no means foreign to Homer—in fact a Homeric simile closely parallels it (*Il.* 15.80–83)—but its incorporation into this *ekphrasis,* or artifact-description, is nevertheless a beautiful and suggestive adaptation of the traditional material.

Outrageous beyond anything we can imagine in a Homeric ekphrasis is the repeated claim that the shield of Herakles can be heard as well as seen. We know that the simultaneous assault on all the senses is characteristic of Hesiodic style, and the present passage is a consistent extension of that style. The feet of the running Gorgons make the shield resound (231–33)—much as, later in the poem when the narrative has returned to the duel itself, an enormous landscape expanded and enriched with toponyms resounds to the cries of the heroes (380–82).

One of the most remarkable passages within the description of the shield is the account of the city at war, where the battle descriptions clearly anticipate the duel to come. Both the Homeric and the Hesiodic shields are organized to interact thematically with the poems in which they are situated; in both the contrast of war and peace is poignant and of an exceptionally immediate relevance. But simply because of the difference of scale, the integration of the Hesiodic shield into its context is more easily appreciable and, I would argue, more ingenious. The shield *is* the battle about to occur, and what it conveys includes the consequences of battle, depicted with extraordinary horror and expanded to cosmic dimensions. The climax comes with the figure of *Akhlys*, the mist that closes over the eyes in death (I have borrowed the translation "Deathmist" from Lattimore), another of the personifications first developed in the Hesiodic corpus:

> And there stood gloomy and terrible Deathmist,
> pallid and dessicated, bent double with hunger,
> joints swollen. Her fingers bore long claws.
> Mucus dripped from her nostrils, and from her cheeks
> blood dripped to the ground. She grinned
> incessantly, and heaps of dust lay over her shoulders,
> muddied with tears.
>
> [264–70]

This remarkable image stands at the juncture between the description of the city at war and that of the city at peace— again the stark juxtaposition, again the extraordinarily daring language. The word translated "mucus" above (*muksai*) occurs nowhere else in poetry—it is otherwise confined to the medical literature—and its choice here gives us an idea of the aberrant mannerism of this poetic style.

At the end of the description of the shield, when we have reached the rim and the streams of Ocean, an unmistakably Hesiodic detail returns us to the larger context of the duel with Kyknos. Homer's Ocean was empty—an easily imagined wave motif all around the outermost register of the shield. Hesiod's is populated by swans (*kyknoi*), swans that fly above it and swim in it, swans that can be heard calling (316–17).

If we have given this little poem so much attention here,

it is because it is at once quite accessible—its organization is clearer than that of any other poem in the corpus—and because it communicates so vividly some of the most striking characteristics of that corpus. In attempting to characterize the difference between this Hesiodic account of heroic warfare and the Homeric passages that invite comparison with it, Hermann Fränkel (1975, 112) evokes the visions of war in the paintings of Goya. The comparison is a telling one, first because the *Shield* does embody the grotesque and upsetting violence that is inseparable from Goya's images. Beyond the revealing similarities, though, it is interesting that we tend to look to recent artistic representations in search of comparisons for Hesiod. This means that we are vastly more conscious here of the presence of a style, an apparently idiosyncratic mode of representation of reality, than we are when we read most Greek poetry. Recent judgments of Hesiod the poet have tended to be harsh: Kirk (1962b, 66) speaks of "futile striving for effect" as well as "awkwardness, repetitiveness, and flaccidity," and West (1966, 307) derides "Hesiod's hobnailed hexameters." All of this is part of the paradox of the Hesiodic corpus, which insists on its individuality and, in fact, delivers an account of the world that is shaped by an aesthetic sensibility in a strikingly individual way. Hesiod's modernity *is* finally his individuality, even if that individuality is a fabrication and a function of a tradition of song rather than an individual singer.

V HESIOD REWRITTEN

Begin thy plowing
When thy Pleiades go down to rest,
Begin thy plowing
40 days are they under seabord,
Thus do in fields by seabord
And in valleys winding down toward the sea.
When the cranes fly high
    think of plowing.
                   —Ezra Pound, "Canto 47"

          That is not dead itself
Which can escape the icy caress of accurate
Memory (and, you might say, make her stuffy, bemused
Daughters buzz off).
          —John Hollander, "A Corona for Wolfgang"

IT IS IMPOSSIBLE TO POINT TO THE MOMENT WHEN HESIOD'S influence began, but there is little doubt that this influence was already felt before the corpus took on its definitive form. In the sixth century B.C., when (assuming that we are correct in assigning a sixth-century date to the *Shield of Herakles*) poets still sang as Hesiod and the corpus could still be expanded, we find the first interactions of the distinctive Hesiodic voice with other poetic voices and the first critiques of Hesiodic ideas and formulations.

The interaction of the Homeric and Hesiodic traditions is

far too pervasive and complex to allow us to speak simply of influence in one direction or the other, though, as we have seen, many passages are complementary (or competitive), and certain fundamental attitudes serve to underline their differences. Characteristically, the Hesiodic voice insists on its individuality—aesthetic and ideological—against the vast, anonymous Homeric backdrop, but if we read this as a strategy of this particular tradition of poetry we cannot take it as a historically reliable indication of the precedence of one tradition over the other. Hesiod does, however, have his place in the progressive individualization of the voice of the poet, a process completed only with the association of the power of poetry with the practical and exploitative power of the tyrants of the sixth century.

The first reactions to Hesiod seem to antedate even this development. What the familiar account of archaic Greek poetry has represented as the first individualized voice *after* Hesiod, the speaker of the Arkhilokhan corpus, is a persona generated to act as the spokesman of the traditional poetry of Paros (Nagy 1979, 304–5; 1982, 50–52). In other words, Arkhilokhos is a myth parallel to the myth of Hesiod.

Arkhilokhos was initiated by the Muses in a bucolic setting, much as was Hesiod. The principal evidence comes from an inscription associated with the hero shrine of Arkhilokhos on Paros, but it is probable that a lost passage of Arkhilokhos closely paralleled the prooimion of the *Theogony.* This is not necessarily a matter of Hesiodic influence on Arkhilokhos— the bucolic initiation is in any case conventional and doubtless far older than either corpus—but it does constitute at the very least a parallelism destined to be read as an interaction. Hesiod and Arkhilokhos are likewise the oldest Greek poetic speakers to incorporate beast fables into their poems, and Arkhilokhos also resembles Hesiod in his use of proverbs.

The parallels were seen in antiquity and are reinforced by abundant verbal echoes. Modern readings affirm that Arkhilokhos is more personal, more concerned with adapting traditional material to the expression of his intimate feelings and experiences. This is certainly what the corpus suggests, but we should bear in mind that confessional poetry in this context is as bound to convention and tradition as wisdom poetry—indeed, this is an excellent example of a situation in which they interact abundantly—and the emerging personae of the sixth century with their increasingly individualized and confessional poses are in this sense extensions of a trend we first perceive in Hesiod. That is perhaps the most important influence of Hesiod on Arkhilokhos: the rudimentary individualization of the shepherd of Helikon as a bearer of the tradition must be seen as the necessary precedent for the more insistent individualization of the persona that spoke the traditions of Paros.

If the forces that generated the individualized personae of sixth-century poetry were interacting with the Hesiodic corpus in a way that contributed to its definition as well as that of other bodies of traditional poetry, the nascent critical-philosophical spirit of Ionia was reacting to Hesiod in a different way. Hesiod's—and Homer's—worst enemy was Xenophanes of Kolophon, whose actual target was of course not the personae that bore the tradition but the tradition itself. He denounced the anthropomorphism of traditional theology with a violence that was to make him dear to the Church Fathers a millennium later, but the ultimate thrust of the Ionian enterprise was clearly the generation of an account of the world that dispensed entirely with gods, regardless of their shape or nature. This Ionian attack on the power of poetic tradition is the clear antecedent of the Sokratic one dramatized by Plato. In both cases, the intensity of the hostility displayed by the enemies of tradition surprises the modern reader. How could it matter so much what the poets said? The reaction itself is finally the best gauge of their power, and this in turn is a further indication that the personae are conventional and mythic. What a blind Khian or a Helikonian shepherd once sang could not possibly carry an authority sufficient to threaten Xenophanes, Pythagoras, Herakleitos, or, later, Sokrates, but the force of traditional lore clearly *could* and did pose such a threat. This Homeric/Hesiodic account of the world had developed sufficient coherence in the hands of its many generations of bearers that, reinforced by the rich trappings of its poetry, it had an authority that the intensely competitive and leveling forces Hesiod himself describes in the account of the "good Strife" would never have conceded to a mere mortal. And yet, armed with a new kind of discourse, the Ionians launched the attack and created a new tradition that effectively demythified Greek cosmology and cosmogony within the short span of two centuries.

The role of Herakleitos should be stressed here, in that he is the first thinker who is known to have reacted not against the poetic power of Hesiod and his anthropomorphic representations of the gods but against the traditional lore itself. It is the Hesiodic pretension to access to vast stores of information (*polymathie*) that Herakleitos attacks, denying that wisdom can be obtained by that route (fr. 40). Herakleitos paradoxically undermines Hesiodic contrasts (fr. 57) and explicitly attacks the *Days*, claiming that in fact there are no lucky or unlucky days—they are all the same (fr. 106). This attack on Hesiod is not directed toward a powerful poet but toward a purveyor of empty superstitions. In Herakleitos's vision, the tradition is a grab bag of forgotten certainties that crumble in our hands.

It is puzzling at first glance that concern with Hesiod

survived the demythifying onslaught of the sixth and fifth centuries. We have seen that Hesiodic themes surface in Aristophanes, and the same is likewise true of Plato, where they clearly represent traditional concerns and value judgments adapted to new contexts, arguments, and aesthetic goals. Perhaps the most striking paradox of the Greek enlightenment is that the theological account of the world represented by the Hesiodic corpus was losing its intellectual credibility during a period when its cultic institutionalization was progressing rapidly. The Olympian cults have Bronze Age antecedents and took on something resembling their classical form by the eighth century B.C. in the Panhellenic shrines of Olympia and Delphi. (As we have already noted, this last development may well be the reason why we have the Homeric and Hesiodic poetry, itself a manifestation of the same cultural change.) But it is the identification of the Olympian cults with the civic life of such cities as Athens during the sixth century that determined the future course of these institutions. By the time of Aristotle, the poetic theology was hopelessly out of date and no longer gave a credible account of the world, but its gods had conspicuous shrines whose rituals were inseparable from the life of the community, and the poems themselves had taken on the respectability accorded by Greek culture automatically to that which was very ancient. Thus Aristotle will occasionally cite Hesiod as he surveys archaic accounts of some matter under consideration, but the authority of tradition rarely impinges on his own search for truth.

Although echoes and adaptations of Hesiod can be found throughout the Greek poetry of the classical period, it was among the poets of Alexandria in the third and second centuries that Hesiod came into his own, and it is their use of him that largely determines our own perceptions of Hesiod the poet. That is, earlier responses to Hesiod are to a greater

or lesser degree competitive responses, whether poetic or
philosophical. Kallimakhos, Apollonios, Theokritos, and their
age were not in any sense threatened by Hesiod, and they
were first and foremost aesthetes with a highly developed
sensitivity to the poses of poets and the manipulation of those
poses. These Hellenistic poets and their reading public—the
first substantial Greek reading public—found in Hesiod perhaps the most sympathetic voice from the archaic period, for
reasons that have already emerged here. Hesiod is insistently
self-referential, he problematizes his own use of language,
and he establishes an ironic distance from his persona. Here
was a poet in the modern (that is, Hellenistic) sense, the principal archaic grounding of a fundamentally new kind of poetry that reveled in the manipulation of convention and was
at the same time intensely retrospective and committed to the
recovery and articulation of ancient lore. For these urbane and
disillusioned scholar-poets, it is of course a matter of manip-
ulating beautiful falsehoods, poses that are the stuff of poetry
and nothing more. But what about Hesiod himself? As I have
suggested, I think we need to resist the temptation to find in
him a ground of authenticity, a level on which what we read
as elegant convention in Hellenistic poetry must somehow be
read as *truth*. For as long as there have been poets there has
been the understanding that their fabrications are lies—beautiful lies if successful, ugly lies if not—and if the Alexandrians
seem to have identified Hesiod more readily than Homer as
their model, I suspect that it was at least in part because they
found in him pre-echoes of their own aestheticism, their own
delight in the play of illusion and convention.

     This is not to say that any of these poets really tried to
do just what Hesiod had done. They were far too sophisticated for that, and they had developed their own elegant and

self-referential styles, their own repertories of poses, in line with contemporary aesthetic sensibilities. But Kallimakhos in particular specifically points to Hesiod as if the archaic poet were the object of his imitation, as if he were setting out explicitly to extend that particular tradition of poetry.

In the surviving poems of Kallimakhos, we find echoes of Hesiodic phrases everywhere, usually in the form of evocations of the Helikonian setting and its springs and nymphs. In the *Aitia* (causes), Kallimakhos steps into Hesiod's place, his Helikonian landscape, to receive instructions from Hesiod's Muses. They are the conventional inspiration, the fictional source, of these explanations of cult practices, local history, and myth strung together into what was once a substantial poem, and though only the broad outlines of the poem can be reconstructed it is clear that it opened and closed with Kallimakhos in the role of Hesiod on Mount Helikon.

In an epigram on the *Phainomena* of Aratos, Kallimakhos extends to his contemporary the same conceit in the form of a compliment—"The song is Hesiod's as well as the manner . . ." (*Ep.* 29.1)—going on to suggest that Aratos had selected "the most honeyed" of Hesiod's diction while avoiding a cruder element. We must assume that Kallimakhos was implicitly comparing Aratos's astronomical poem with the lost *Astronomy* of Hesiod (most of the handful of preserved lines of which come from a scholion on Aratos) rather than the poems known to us. The compliment nevertheless suggests another way in which Hesiod was useful to the Hellenistic poets: he provided an archaic model for a poetics of information and a poetry conceived as a highly decorative surface woven around a content of practical facts. This information might be traditional lore or the latest insights of contemporary science, but in either case its relationship to the poetic medium was arbitrary and problematical. Hesiod's poetry of information provided the precedent for forming the new poetics required.

Far more difficult to specify is the position of Hesiod with reference to the development of the genre of pastoral or bucolic poetry. The idea of a rustic song whose purity and natural inspiration are held up as an aesthetic ideal is often traced beyond Hesiod to the scene on the shield of Akhilleus (*Il.* 18.523–26) where two shepherds play on their pipes in blissful ignorance of the fact that they are about to be slaughtered in an ambush of warriors. Certainly in that ekphrasis the typical contrasts of pastoral are already present—the peaceful idleness of the pastoral life and the latent violence threatening it, the aesthetic ideal of the shepherd as artist and the paradoxical humility of his social status. All of this is conspicuously absent in Hesiod—or rather, it is present only in the provisionally adopted shepherd persona of the *Theogony* prooimion, and even there it is hardly developed. The *Works and Days* provides the principal model and precedent for the genre of agricultural poetry typified by the *Georgics* of Virgil, but this is something else again, a branch of information poetry whose subject matter happens to coincide with that of the central section of Hesiod's poem and is therefore marked as Hesiodic in a special sense. This is not to say that (aside from some isolated passages) the *Georgics* in any meaningful way resemble the *Works and Days* but only that the *ascraeum carmen*, as the *Georgics* designate themselves (2.176), finds its precedent and justification in Hesiod's account of the agricultural year. The complexity of the imitation is vast and deliberately problematized. Virgil imitates Hellenistic information poetry, which in turn imitates Hesiod, and the bard of Askra himself provides the symbolic link guaranteeing the integrity of the tradition.

Even if the "Askraean song" is the *Georgics*, however, Virgil evokes Hesiod himself only in the *Eclogues*, where he clearly appears as the patron of pastoral poetry. This is in the peculiar passage in *Eclogue* 6 (itself a series of paraphrases of songs sung by Silenus) in which Virgil's contemporary Gallus is rather abruptly plopped down next to the Permessos to be taken in hand by Hesiod's Muses and led to an assembly of poets on Mount Helikon, where Linos presents him with the pipes of the "old Askraean" himself. The point of the elegant conceit is clear. The prooimion of the *Theogony* has become the canonical account of the consecration of the poet, and Gallus (who in fact seems to have written for the most part erotic elegiacs) has been accepted as the most recent recruit to the succession that, in this pastoral context, traces its origins to Hesiod. Virgil was of course not the first to evoke the *Theogony* prooimion in pastoral. When the speaker of Theokritos's *Idyll* 7 claims that the Nymphs taught him "many songs as [he] tended cattle in the mountains," the reference is clear. Hesiod, it seems, could be invoked as the founder of both traditions of poetry about rustic things. His account of the consecration of the poet could be generalized to cover any sort of poet, and its bucolic trappings gave him a special place in the (pre-)history of pastoral as it developed in Hellenistic and Roman poetry.

We have already seen that Hesiod was not ideally served by the manuscript tradition. Much that was considered Hesiodic was lost, in part at least for lack of continuing interest. When the great medievalist Ernst Robert Curtius wrote that "Hesiod put so much instruction into his work that, as a poet, he has had nothing to say to later times," he undoubtedly represented at least the medieval reception of Hesiod with some accuracy. The meaning of Hesiod (like that of Homer) had passed largely into the hands of the mystical allegorists in late antiquity, and as the interpretations repeated from the second-century Platonist Kelsos by his Christian adversary Origen show, it was possible to read Hesiodic theology as an archaic, anticipatory encoding of the theology of later Platonism. Pagan allegorical readings of Homer gave way relatively peacefully to Christian readings, but this new dominant interpretive community found little of value in Hesiod, now stripped of any vestige of theological authority.

Before 1450 Hesiod was virtually unknown in Italy, but by the end of the fifteenth century the *Works and Days* came to be one of the Greek works best represented in the libraries of the humanists. The first Latin translation appeared in 1471, and Hesiod was also one of the first Greek authors to receive a printed edition. Bound, significantly, with Theokritos, Hesiod was the second author printed by Aldus Manutius in Florence after his press was set up in 1494. Vernacular translations came more slowly, though, before 1600 only in France, where Ronsard and the Pléiade, the literary vanguard of northern Europe, made considerable (if largely decorative) use of Hesiod.

In England, pastoral flourished in the sixteenth century, and Spenser, imitating the Pléiade, in turn imitated and even translated Virgil. In his version of "Virgils Gnat," Spenser colorfully expands Virgil's unadorned reference to the "Askraean poet" (96) into "that Ascraean bard whose fame now rings / Through the wide world." Spenser's *Shepheardes Calender*, though, in spite of the obvious relevance of the Hesiodic model, has little that smacks of Hesiod. The mysterious contemporary commentator "E.K." glosses "silver song" (*April* 46), saying that it "seemeth to imitate the lyke in Hesiodus ἀργυρέον μέλος," but the phrase is not Hesiodic (nor does *melos* ever refer to song in Homer or Hesiod). Moreover, for the Muses and their attributes (as for most other ancient lore)

E.K.'s preferred authority is Virgil, not Hesiod, and it is explicitly Virgil, Theokritos, and Mantuan who are the major models here.

If Chapman's translation of Hesiod (1618) has not inspired the retrospective ecstasies his Homer provoked in Keats, one reason is undoubtedly that it has been much less read. The title is revealing in spite of its long-windedness:

> The GEORGICKS of HESIOD; by George Chapman; TRANS-LATED ELABORATELY out of the Greek: Containing Doctrine of Husbandrie, Moralitie, and Pietie; with a perpetuall Calendar of Good and Bad Daies; Not superstitious, but necessarie (as farre as naturall Causes compell) for all Men obserue, and difference in following their affaires.

Chapman clearly intended his audience to read Hesiod *through* Virgil—the Virgilian title created a familiar context for this aberrant and often obscure text. He divided the *Works and Days* into three "Georgics," the introduction, the farming lore, and the *Days*, into the last of which he inserted a wonderful Hesiodic fragment preserved in Plutarch on the longevity of various real and fabulous animals (fr. 304). This curious work, clearly if hopelessly packaged as viable information that the reader could actually put to use, was dedicated to Francis Bacon and sported congratulatory verses by Michael Drayton and Ben Jonson. Even for one who can admire Chapman's Homer, this translation presses hard on the limits of readability, the text cluttered with numbers referring to a vast array of marginal notes. And yet it was *the* English Hesiod for a long time—no competitors rushed to defy Jonson's warning in his congratulatory poem against trespassing on Chapman's turf before Thomas Cooke, who translated both poems in 1728.

Although there was still no translation of the *Theogony*, Hesiod was not neglected in seventeenth-century England. The post-Renaissance poet who has taken Hesiod most seriously may well be John Milton. Only the *Works and Days* was easily accessible to the English reading public in Milton's time, but early readers of *Paradise Lost* pointed repeatedly to parallel passages in the *Theogony*. It has recently been argued that Milton deliberately and systematically rewrites the titanomachy in the central portion of *Paradise Lost* (Porter 1982). That Milton knew and chose to compete with the poetic theology of the Greeks is well known, but what this recent work suggests is an openness toward and respect for the adversary that go beyond what had previously been claimed. This ambivalent attitude toward the Greek theogony was passed on, as we shall see, to Milton's self-appointed spiritual heir, William Blake.

The decline of the pastoral genre in the eighteenth century coincided with the rediscovery of mythology as a reservoir of imaginative material and usable cultural data. It is that rebirth of interest in myth that has guaranteed Hesiod a reading public for the past two centuries and continues to do so. By the nineteenth century, in the context of European literature, Hesiod the poet was reduced to a few reusable symbols. None were generally read as specifically Hesiodic, but they had once been the exclusive property of his tradition.

Preeminent among these symbols are the Helikonian Muses, with whom we can close our account of Hesiod's influence. Hesiod's voice, identified as the manifestation of the Muses' wisdom, became for Milton and then, more explicitly, for Blake, the representative of Greek poetic tradition, its successes and its failures. The eighteenth century had largely stripped away the baggage of traditional allegorical interpretation with which Homer had returned to the Western European tradition, and Pope had produced a translation of Homer that admirably recreated the *Iliad* and *Odyssey* for his age. Like all recreations of Homer, it is a remythification or, to put it more generously, an appreciation, and a brilliant one. Hesiod was not so fortunate and remained an odd but representative figure—the spokesman for the claims of the Greek tradition, but now a persona without a poem, the visionary shepherd-poet, but virtually unread.

Blake's famous manifesto in his preface to *Milton* has been evoked above (p. 64):

> [W]hen the New Age is at leisure to Pronounce, all will be set right, & those Grand Works of the more ancient & consciously & professedly Inspired Men will hold their proper rank, & the Daughters of Memory shall become the Daughters of Inspiration. . . . We do not want either Greek or Roman models if we are but just & true to our own Imaginations.

That would seem to dispose of Hesiod by disposing of his link to poetic power and authority. The Daughters of Memory are the grounding of the "Stolen and Perverted Writings of Homer & Ovid, of Plato & Cicero," the servants of the corrupted tradition and of imperialist militarism, the enemies of vision. Their replacement by the Daughters of Inspiration is Blake's representation of the poetry of Milton, conceived as the victory over the tradition of Greece and Rome of a Christianity that is in fact the aesthetic religion of the visionary imagination. Sensitive readers of Blake, including Northrop Frye, have done something to restore our perspective here (in spite of Blake himself) and to show the affinities of Blake's enterprise to Hesiod's. If we read Hesiod himself along the lines I have suggested, the affinities become, I think, even clearer. Behind Blake's contempt for the Daughters of Memory lies a deep community of purpose and spirit with the Hesiodic corpus—an uncompromising and insistent declaration of the power of poetry to shape and articulate the fundamental givens of our universe.

What follows is fragmented as the tradition of poetry is fragmented—most problematically, in the modernism of Ezra Pound, whose rewriting of Hesiod has already been mentioned. There are a few actual flashes of translation of Hesiod in the *Cantos*, including the one quoted as epigraph to this chapter. But the cranky Helikonian peasant is always standing among the other ghosts of the tradition at Pound's shoulder, as the personal and the global, the political and the theological are stirred together into the *Cantos'* endless monologue for many voices. Still, the lovely ironies of John Hollander's "Corona for Wolfgang" (the second epigraph above) offer a more appropriate closing word. A rewriting of Blake, of course, rather than Hesiod himself, they give us Hesiod's distance as well as his immediacy, his absorption in the only tradition that offers us the opportunity of reading him as a poet, and the stubborn resistance to the erosion of time of that first European assertion of the identity and function of the poet.

BIBLIOGRAPHY

THE ESSENTIAL MODERN COMMENTARIES ON THE *THEOGONY* AND THE *Works and Days* are those of M. L. West (1966; 1978). Each contains a wealth of information and analysis easily accessible not only to the intended philological readership but also to those who make no use of the accompanying Greek text. Specific questions and problems are more likely to be resolved here than elsewhere. West (1985) has also discussed the *Catalogue of Women*.

For fresh and innovative discussion of the development of archaic Greek poetry, see Gregory Nagy (1979) as well as Nagy's introductory article on Hesiod (1982), and for a challenging and insightful reading of Hesiod, Piero Pucci (1977).

More conservative in approach, the following general surveys are also extremely valuable: Friedrich Solmsen (1949) and the chapter on Hesiod in Hermann Fränkel (1975). Very enlightening on the *Theogony* is G. S. Kirk (1962b).

By way of background, the basic studies of the relationship of archaic Greek poetry to oral tradition are G. S. Kirk (1962a) and A. B. Lord (1960).

Beyond these general works, I have made reference in the text to a handful of articles that represent current trends in the study of Hesiod. The problem of the personal versus the collective is well treated by Mark Griffith (1983). Jean-Pierre Vernant (1983) throws light on the Hesiodic myth of the successive races of mankind. Much of the best work on the sexual politics of Hesiod has appeared in *Arethusa*, the liveliest current journal concerned with ancient literature. See especially Marilyn B. Arthur (1982; 1983), Nicole Loraux (1978), and Linda S. Sussman (1978).

P. W. Wallace (1974) discusses the sites and monuments of the valley of the Arkhontitsa, and William Malin Porter (1982) clarifies one of the most important phases of Hesiod's influence on modern poetry in his study of Milton's use of Hesiod.

The Derveni cosmogony still awaits definitive publication, but a helpful discussion can be found in G. S. Kirk, J. E. Raven, and M. Schofield (1983). On Theognis, see Andrew L. Ford (1985) and the other articles in the same volume. Finally, the closely comparable passages from the Theogony and the Odyssey discussed in chapter 1 are explored in greater depth and situated in the larger tradition of poetry of instruction by Richard P. Martin (1984).

Translations of some of the archaic poets I have compared with Hesiod—including Theognis, Semonides, and Anakreon—are most easily available in Richmond Lattimore (1960).

Arthur, Marilyn B. 1982. "Cultural Strategies in Hesiod's Theogony: Law, Family, and Society." Arethusa 15:63–82.

————. 1983. "The Dream of a World without Women: Poetics and Circles of Order in the Theogony Prooemium." Arethusa 16:97–116.

Ford, Andrew L. 1985. "The Seal of Theognis: The Politics of Authorship in Ancient Greece." In Theognis of Megara. Edited by Thomas J. Figuera and Gregory Nagy. Baltimore: Johns Hopkins University Press.

Fränkel, Hermann. 1975. Early Greek Poetry and Philosophy. New York: Harcourt, Brace, Jovanovich.

Griffith, Mark. 1983. "Personality in Hesiod." Classical Antiquity 2:37–65.

Kirk, G. S. 1962a. The Songs of Homer. Cambridge: Cambridge University Press.

————. 1962b. "The Structure and Aims of the Theogony." In Hésiode et son influence, 61–107. Entretiens Hardt 7. Geneva: Fondation Hardt.

Kirk, G. S., J. E. Raven, and M. Schofield. 1983. The Presocratic Philosophers. 2d ed. Cambridge: Cambridge University Press.

Lattimore, Richmond, trans. 1960. Greek Lyrics. 2d ed. Chicago: University of Chicago Press.

Loraux, Nicole. 1978. "Sur la race des femmes et quelques-unes de ses tribus." Arethusa 11:43–89.

Lord, A. B. 1960. The Singer of Tales. Cambridge, Mass.: Harvard University Press.

Martin, Richard P. 1984. "Hesiod, Odysseus, and the Instruction of Princes." *Transactions of the American Philological Association* 114:29–48.

Nagy, Gregory. 1979. *The Best of the Achaeans*. Baltimore: Johns Hopkins University Press.

———. 1982. "Hesiod." In *Ancient Authors*. Edited by T. J. Luce. New York: Scribner's.

Porter, William Malin. 1982. "A View from 'Th' Aonian Mount': Hesiod and Milton's Critique of the Classics." *Classical and Modern Literature* 3:5–23.

Pucci, Piero. 1977. *Hesiod and the Language of Poetry*. Baltimore: Johns Hopkins University Press.

Solmsen, Friedrich. 1949. *Hesiod and Aeschylus*. Ithaca, N.Y.: Cornell University Press.

Sussman, Linda S. 1978. "Workers and Drones: Labor, Idleness, and Gender Definition in Hesiod's Beehive." *Arethusa* 11:27–41.

Vernant, Jean-Pierre. 1983. *Myth and Thought among the Greeks*. London: Routledge and Kegan Paul.

Wallace, P. W. 1974. "Hesiod and the Valley of the Muses." *Greek, Roman, and Byzantine Studies* 15:5–24.

West, M. L. 1966. *Hesiod: Theogony*. Oxford: Oxford University Press.

———. 1978. *Hesiod: Works and Days*. Oxford: Oxford University Press.

———. 1985. *The Hesiodic Catalogue of Women: Its Nature, Structure, and Origins*. Oxford: Oxford University Press.

TRANSLATIONS

As of 1987, there are available two recent verse translations of all three major poems of Hesiod, two more that omit the *Shield of Herakles,* and finally Norman O. Brown's prose translation of the *Theogony*—an old standby. In this book I have used my own translations, which are unashamedly adapted to whatever point the citation in question was meant to serve. The problem of deciding which translation to rely on is an important one, though, and what follows is intended to serve as an introduction to the strengths and weaknesses of the most popular versions of Hesiod.

First, a word about Evelyn-White's prose translation in the Loeb edition, with facing Greek. I have a strong sentimental attachment to this little volume, a unique attachment, since the Loebs are for the most part a drab and unlovable lot. But the Loeb Hesiod served me years ago in making my way through the poems at a time when my Greek was far from equal to the task. True, Evelyn-White's English is simply another modulation of the anonymous Edwardian singsong that is the poetic language of the Loeb Classical Library. It is prose that just cannot resist the temptation to run to dactyls ("Good is she also when men contend at the games . . . there too the goddess is with them and profits them"). But, the refinements of several generations of scholarship aside, it is accurate enough. And you get so much! Along with the three major poems there are the more substantial fragments of the

Catalogue of Women and the other largely lost works that went
under Hesiod's name . . . *and* the Homeric *Hymns* and everything else that went under Homer's name, except the *Iliad*
and *Odyssey*, with the *Contest of Homer and Hesiod* thrown in
to round it off. So there are good reasons for making use of
Evelyn-White, especially if you have a smattering of Greek
(or even an ambition to have a smattering of Greek)—but the
thought that a reader might take Evelyn-White's prose as a
viable equivalent for the voice of Hesiod in the waning years
of the twentieth century makes my blood run cold.

Of the four verse translations, two are recent and contemporaries (1983)—Frazer (without the *Shield*) and Athanassakis—another, Dorothea Wender's 1973 Penguin edition,
also omits the *Shield* and is bound with a translation of Theognis, and the fourth (Lattimore 1959), has, through some bizarre marketing strategy of the University of Michigan Press,
never been published in paperback.

R. M. Frazer did us all a great service in the 1960s by
bringing out a fresh, accessible translation of Dares and Dictys, the late "supplements" to Homer. The Hesiod is less exciting. The unfortunate decision to offer "an approximation
of the dactylic hexameter of the original" leaves us with a
lilting singsong:

> Good is she too whenever the athletes compete in the
>   games,
> where for whomever this goddess is present, granting
>   him aid. . . .

The serious English dactyl did not survive "the forest
primeval"—though in the humorous mode it has a rich tradition ("Higgledy, piggledy . . ."). Beyond this, Frazer's strategy of interrupting the poems with italicized prose "comments," though aimed at elucidating the often obscure train

of thought, tends rather to break the poetry into a jumble of fragments.

Apostolos Athanassakis's translations of all three poems are a good deal better. Though they accept at face value much internal evidence that I read as convention and poetic play, the introductions are concise and vivid, and the notes (for the few who will make full use of them) extremely helpful and sometimes quite beautiful. Listen to the refreshing straightforwardness of our sample lines in this version:

> Again, she is a noble goddess when men compete
> for athletic prizes, because she stands by them and
> helps. . . .

This is a recognizable American equivalent for the language of Hesiod—strong, confident, unhackneyed, and innovative in its rhythms.

Dorothea Wender's Penguin version approaches the problem of translating Hesiod in an entirely different way. She simply adopts the most pedestrian and transparent of traditional English meters—blank verse—and with that formal mark to establish the distance of this discourse from prose, offers a very competent translation, sticking closely to the Greek. It is not exciting poetry—it does not aspire to be, and Wender makes it clear that she has little respect for Hesiod's "style" (especially that "rather poor piece of work" the *Shield*, omitted, perhaps fortunately, here). But this translation inspires confidence and on the whole is quite readable, even if the reader risks coming out of it a little shaken by the washboard effect of her insistent iambs. Here is our arbitrarily chosen pair of lines from the Hekate hymn:

> A splendid ally in the games, when men
> Compete, then, too, she brings success and help.

But listen now to Richmond Lattimore:

> She is great, too,
>   where men contend in athletics,
> and there the goddess stands by those
>   whom she will, and assists them. . . .

Lattimore's Hesiod fell chronologically between his *Iliad* and his *Odyssey* but resembles neither. His renderings of Homer often strike me as stiff and ponderous, far too faithful to the Greek to be read as English poetry, but for this reason dear to philologists when they find themselves in the position of teaching Homer in translation. But even if it, too, is occasionally overliteral, his Hesiod is his great achievement. The idea of printing the *Works and Days* on the right page only with the left reserved for an extremely concise summary in the form of gnomic scholia was an inspired one. Any reader in any language will be lost in the maze of abrupt transitions in that poem, and Lattimore's solution is masterful. The translation contains some inexplicable lapses—his Muses give Hesiod "olive," not laurel!—but his poetry is still the best. Finally, though Athanassakis also has extensive indices, Lattimore's are more useful, and only Lattimore's translation includes a graph summarizing the generations of the *Theogony*.

In a sense, our problem in assessing these translations is really an aspect of a larger problem that has come up repeatedly in this study, that of the *use* of Hesiod. Homer has been more fortunate than Hesiod in the sense that his poems have been read, in modern times at least, primarily as stories, sagas, tales that have no definitive form beyond what he gives us. In the Middle Ages it was a commonplace that Dares and Dictys gave the *historical* account of the Trojan War, while Homer and Virgil had other motives for telling the story as they did, aesthetic (or political) motives. Hence Homer has had a better chance of being read for his own sake than Hesiod, who has commonly been read for access to something beyond. In the *Theogony*, readers have sought an authentic and canonical archaic Greek theology. In the *Works and Days*, they have sought authentic and reliable information on the rural society and economy of the dark age on the threshold of archaic Greece. All the poetic translations make attempts to go beyond this use of Hesiod, at least to the extent that they present themselves as poetic equivalents to Hesiod's Greek. Their success is uneven, and such translations have at best a short shelf life, but if Hesiod is to live on as a poet it can only be in the medium of poetry, however difficult the transitions required. The best of these verse translations are wonderful poetry, and every one has brilliant moments, when through some unexpected adjustment of sound and sense a turn of phrase suddenly illuminates the underlying Greek and makes Hesiod speak our language.

The last translation we need to consider, Norman O. Brown's prose *Theogony*, has been in print continuously for more than thirty years. As one expects from its author, the introduction is full of sharp insights that are still fresh and suggestive. It makes no pretense to recreating the poetic artifact but gives us a vigorous and readable prose version that is manifestly for *use*, to allow us to penetrate the poem for the evidence that it has to yield concerning early Greek myth. If that is the goal—and without the Greek, any more ambitious one is highly elusive—Brown's *Theogony* is probably still the one to read. Still, if asked point blank which English Hesiod is best, I recommend Lattimore's.

Here are the available translations:

Athanassakis: Hesiod. *Theogony, Works and Days, Shield*. Translation, introduction, and notes by Apostolos N. Athanas-sakis. Baltimore: Johns Hopkins University Press, 1983.

Brown: Hesiod. *Theogony.* Translated with an introduction by Norman O. Brown. The Library of the Liberal Arts. Indianapolis: Bobbs-Merrill, 1953.

Evelyn-White: *Hesiod, The Homeric Hymns and Homerica.* With an English translation by Hugh G. Evelyn-White. Loeb Classical Library. London and Cambridge: Heinemann and Harvard University Press, 1914.

Frazer: *The Poems of Hesiod.* Translated with introduction by R. M. Frazer. Norman: University of Oklahoma Press, 1983.

Lattimore: *Hesiod.* Translated by Richmond Lattimore. Ann Arbor: University of Michigan Press, 1959.

Wender: *Hesiod and Theognis.* Translated with an introduction by Dorothea Wender. Harmondsworth: Penguin, 1973.

INDEX